The THEORETICAL TIGER SOCIETY

poems by BRIAN FUCHS

with contributions by Robert A. Cozzi, Jairo Dealba, Max Asbeek Brusse, Jarrod Hol, Cheryl Couture, Justin Ward, & Kerith Hawkins.

Edited by Jairo Dealba.

☛ SCISSORTAIL PRESS ☚
STILLWATER, OKLAHOMA

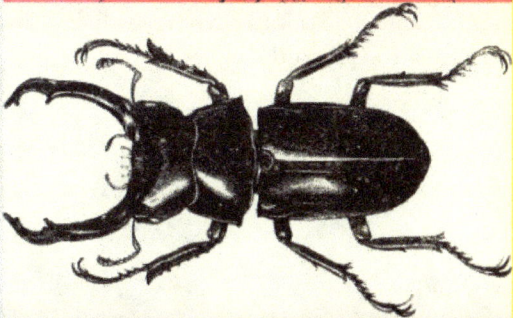

ADVANCE PRAISE FOR THE THEORETICAL TIGER SOCIETY

"In The Theoretical Tiger Society, Fuchs bestows upon the reader an intimate mosaic of words that invite the reader into the most personal corners of his mind."

–Robert A. Cozzi

"Our paths crossed many years ago. Poetry was the link that connected us. Over the years I kept a distant eye on what Brian was writing. It came as a huge surprise when he asked me to read his collection of poems. Reading his words reminded me of our connection and the strength in his work. We both use our work as our autobiography. Brian Fuchs let's us into his world with honesty, intimacy, love, lust and humanity. His story is unique. We will find facets of ourselves in his observations and definitions. He is a man full of life."

–Paul Lorenz

"The Theoretical Tiger Society is another beautiful poetry collection by Brian Fuchs. It oozes the same sensual lyrical images of his other works, but is somehow heavier in its delivery, like bold impasto strokes on a blank canvas. From the yards of soft peach chiffon that weave through the book to steamy encounters of lust and sex, there is something sweet and endearing about this vulnerable coming-of-age journey of self-acceptance and self-love."

–Lisa Bain

"The Theoretical Tiger Society…has and is the essence of what it means to root and to branch out into the world of poetics. Fuchs has invited me to think differently…in an open-hearted path that leads me to understand the heart of a poet. …He has cheered me on all the way through the book, helping me see with his magnanimous poetry that it is possible to break free from the chains of what it means to be a poet and tell [one's] truth."

–Jairo Dealba

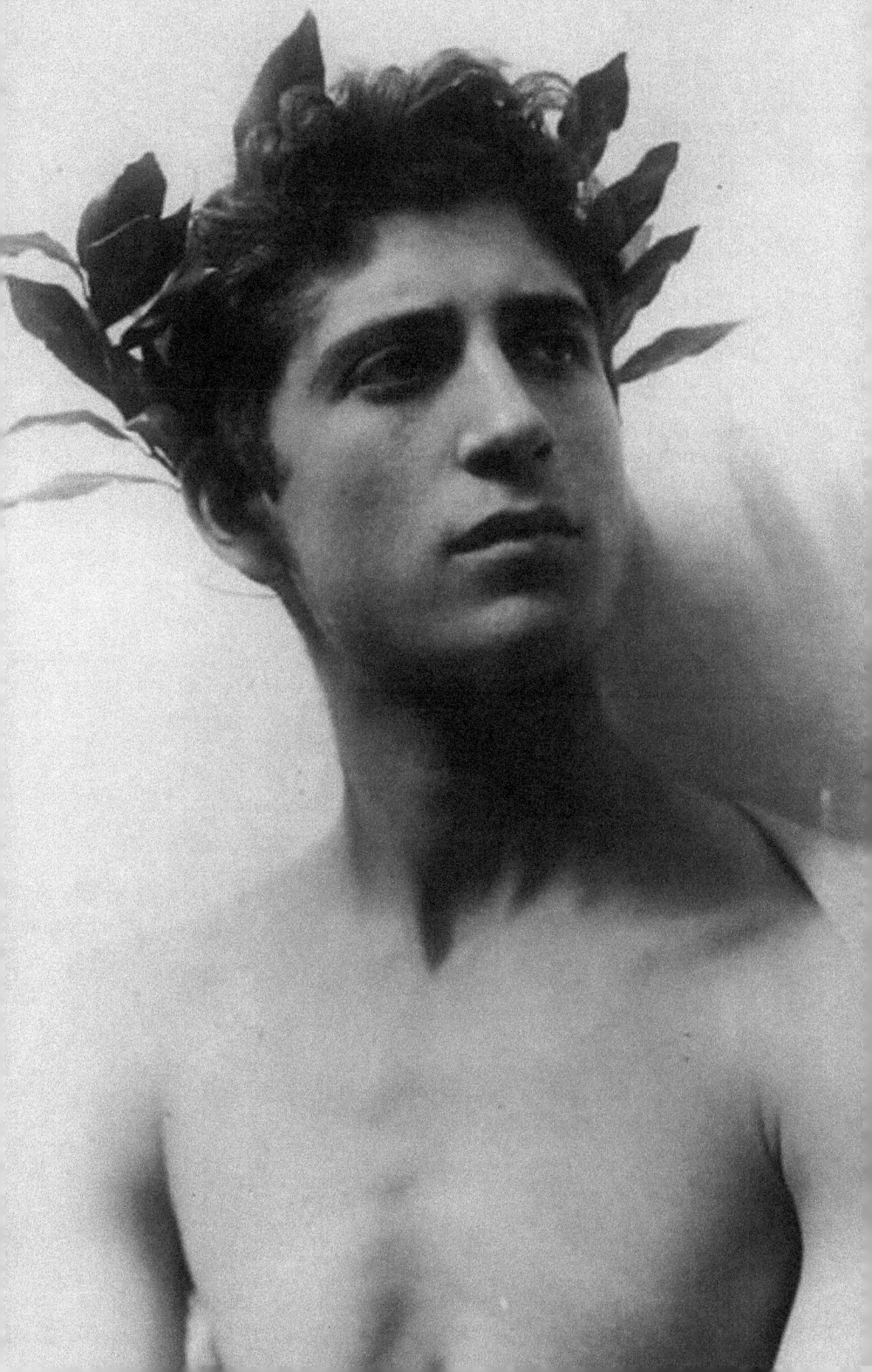

Paperback (Color) ISBN: 978-1-955814-79-9
Paperback (B&W) ISBN: 978-1-955814-78-2

Edited by Jairo Dealba

Book design by Brian Fuchs
www.brianfuchs.com

Scissortail Press
scissortailpress.com
4500 E Burris Rd
Glencoe, OK 74032
USA

☿

Sing!
transparent to the light
    through which the light
shines, through the stone,
    until
the stone-light glows,
    pink jade
—that is the light and is
    a stone
and is a church—if the image
    hold...
and at a breath a face glows
    and fades!
Come all ye aberrant,
    drunks, prostitutes,
    Surrealists—
    Gide and—
Proust's memory (in a cork
    diving suit
looking under the sea
            of silence)
to bear witness: [1]

—William Carlos Williams, "The Pink Church"

CONTENTS

ACKNOWLEDGMENTS   x v

A LULLABY FOR DEER   0 1
PEACH CHIFFON   0 2
IT WAS THEN MY EYES   0 4
DAWN   0 6
ELEPHANTS   0 7
CHURCH   0 9
FIREWORKS   1 0
TOLL COLLECTOR AT THE BARN   1 1
TRYST   1 3
A BREATHLESS SOLITUDE   1 4
      WITH ROBERT A. COZZI
THE CRAFTING OF WORDS REVEALS   1 5
PARTLY CLOUDY   1 6
EVERY MOON HANGS IN THE NIGHT   1 7
DUST   1 9
BOX OF COLORS   2 0
THE FABRIC OF HIS SHIRT   2 1
TIGERS   2 3
PIANO PLAYER AT THE GYPSY   2 7
      COFFEE HOUSE
AUSTIN, TEXAS   3 0
PLUTO PROJECTOR   3 2
NECTAR   3 4
      WITH JUSTIN WARD
YOUR BEAUTY IN FEBRUARY   3 5
YOUR BEAUTY IN APRIL   3 7

WHITE   38
    WITH CHERYL COUTURE
THE NEXT MORNING   39
INSTAGRAM   40
HOW MUCH TIME DID YOUR CREATION TAKE   43
PEN-D-ULES   46
NAKED BODIES   48
LES SOUVENIRS DE PETIT GARÇON   50
PENANCE FOR MY CRIMES   53
PHANTOM   54
A CONFESSION   55
TURTLES ALL THE WAY DOWN   57
BEFORE I DROWN   58
FAG(GOT   61
THE SNOW IN HER EYES   64
ANNEMARIE IS DOING HER LAUNDRY   67
FOR ROBERT Q. LEWIS   70
CHRISTMAS BLUE   71
HONEYSUCKLE   72
DANIEL, ON HIS BIRTHDAY   73
IMMORTALITY   74
PROFFERS THE MEANING OF THE STARS   75
EXTINCTION   77
MY FIRST   81
FRAGMENTS IN THE RAIN   82
    WITH MAX ABEEK BRUSSE & JARROD HOL
REQUIEM FOR MYSELF   85
MOONLIGHT DISTRACTIONS   88
AURAS   89
GOLDENROD   91
DEAD OF NIGHT   94
A TRUE ACCOUNT OF TALKING TO THE SUN   95
    AT FIRE ISLAND
I'D LIKE HIM TO WEAR BOOTS   97
TULIP-KING   98
KEVIN HAWKINS   100

IS SAND & STARS   101
WITH KERITH HAWKINS
A WILD WOMAN   104
LAWRENCE FERLINGHETTI IS DEAD   107
MARCONA ALMONDS   114
THE CIRCLE BY JAIRO DEALBA   116
INVISIBLE SPIDERS   117
A KALEIDOSCOPE   118
SKIN   121
LIGHTNING BUGS   122
NOSTALGIC STRAGGLE   123
A TIGER; A CORSAIR; A LAMB   124
A SLICE OF PUMPKIN PIE   125
DISCOVERING YOUR BOTANY   127
FAIRY BOY   129
NOCTURNE   132
HOP OFF, LITTLE LAPIN   135
A NEW CLOAK FOR THE OCCASION   137
MANGO-HEARTED KING   141
SPECIAL   142
MINOTAUR   145
A THEORY OF TIGERS   151

AFTERWORD   154
ABOUT THE AUTHOR   157
IMAGE CREDITS   158
ENDNOTES   162

ACKNOWLEDGMENTS

A few notes on specific members of THE THEORETICAL TIGER SOCIETY who have helped in the creation of this book.

There are a few people whose encouragement and support have been instrumental in the process. It would not exist without them. Thank you for everything to
JAIRO DEALBA, ROBERT A. COZZI, BRENT FUCHS, & JUSTIN WARD

Without the fantastic collaborations from the creative minds of some amazing writers, this book would not be the same. Thank you for the words to
KERITH HAWKINS, MAX ASBEEK BRUSSE, JARROD HOL, & CHERYL COUTURE

A few people are constant sources of inspiration. Some I have known for decades, and others have passed through my life briefly, but I hold them in my heart as fondly. Thank you for being my eternal muses to
DANIEL NARANJO, TRAVIS LATHAM, J.D. WINTERHALTER, WESLEYAN FORAKER, SKYLAR AREND, PAUL LORENZ,

KAMERON ROBINSON, ANGELA LIBAL, KEVIN HAWKINS, SCOTT MALOLEY, JERRY FAIRCHILD, & JENNIE LLOYD

Thanks you to some of the people who sparked my love of poetry and my belief in my own words.
CURTIS FUCHS, D.B. WRIGHT, MELISSA STEINLE, FRANK SESSO, EMILY SALT, LISA BAIN, BRADLEY FUCHS, CHRISTINE PEREZ, HEATHER ARONNO, JESSICA POWERS, & JULIE SEVILLA DRAKE

A few bits of love for those whose memory guides me daily. Thank you for the many wonderful times to
LADONNA FUCHS, JOHN HAYNES, JOBETH JOHNSTON, MARY COMBS, COLBY WEDMAN, BETTICUS DIXON, & CHARLES   HART

A Lullaby for Deer

Hush now, restless creatures,
let your woodland hooves rest
in a thicket of soft bushes;
the night is moving toward us
over the still horizon.

Each eyelash connects
to a waiting dream,
tender leaves on each
branch through the night,
a lush meadow at dawn
where you'll frolic until your
spots begin to fade.

Hush now, sweet deer,
back to the forests,
back to your mama's side.
It's time for you to sleep.

for Kai

24 JULY 2021 — PAYNE COUNTY, OKLAHOMA

PEACH CHIFFON

7.

I put on the nightgown,

              peach chiffon and marabou.

In
that
moment

my secrets erupted, spilled out into the rented living room, seeped into the brown carpet, in a moment's full glory. Everything was possible. Flames shot from my awkward fingers, my so often unfamiliar skin charged and overheated.

              I danced.

That sheer fabric slipped over my skin, melting away those lessons I'd learned in masculinity, dissolving the smell of Brüt, Old Spice, shaving cream, menthol cigarettes, cheap beer. Ashtrays. The smell of men mumbling about their horrible lives, their inadequacies, their disinterested wives. The smell of dusty halls where it was never easy to dance, where I could never find a place to let my hips swish as they had always wanted to.

I was joy.

I danced there
free from judgement,
free from side-eyes,
free from the dramatic clutching of pearls.

I was joy.

Pearls! Pearls would have been perfect, clutched or otherwise, draped over the feathers. Perfect, if not a bit extra. I never did mind being a little extra, not until I saw those side-eyes, and felt the burst of dust in my face as those mumbling old men banged their old books at me.

In my grandma's eyes I could see snow,

a fading joy.
Solitude.

16 APRIL 2008 — ANCHORAGE, ALASKA
A VERSION ORIGINALLY APPEARED IN *SOCIAL DISTANCES* (2020)

IT WAS THEN MY EYES

opened
in a fullness of knowledge
a juvenile epiphany

it was then I found myself
pebbles behind
undisturbed elms
nestled through timid
unvisited woods

04

& I knew
the limits of secrets
the futility of honesty
the subtle importance of fear

patches of uneaten grass
life-cycling alone in a clearing
wandering with the planets
through the unsettling
stillness of space

little boys are
so good at never being
truly themselves
when being those selves
draws all light from the sun
to spotlight every breath

a deer skeleton
flushed green in
the moist undergrowth
the pale fluorescence
of luna moth wings left
falling gently at dusk

6 JUNE 2021 — PAYNE COUNTY, OKLAHOMA

DAWN

The sky burned pink this morning,
shining through the glass baubles
Mom had hung in the kitchen window,
to capture rainbows
& throw them across the walls.

I'm so tired of never being the right man,
of being so stuck in a past that never wanted
for any of us to shine our bright lights through,
& have our moms track the rainbows across the walls.
I'm tired of having to realize how tired I've been.

I burned pink this morning,
flew with the crows
before the yellowing of the sun's rays,

to futures I can only imagine,
where the rainbows can creep across my skin,
and the fires beneath the surface are allowed
to erupt into the glorious fires
they have always been.

I'm waiting to catch Apollo's eye,
to be loved so much that he creates

new flowers
from my spilled blood.

30 MAY 2021 — PAYNE COUNTY, OKLAHOMA

ELEPHANTS

Tiptoeing
slipping in — and
out —
the windows seal
themselves shut,
rust & warp.
We felt each other,
came to life
before we were ready.
So much is riding
on the backs
of elephants.
Words dance merrily
around the point,
slipping in — and
out —
translucence stares
back through mirrors.
I close my eyes.
It's easier to slip past,
ignore,
wait silently for
acknowledgement.
I'm trying to feel
around for my form,
shrinking back,
impaling myself
on tusks.

17 FEBRUARY 2009 — ANCHORAGE, ALASKA

CHURCH

I wanted silence,
I wanted my eyes
to behave,
to stop my sex
from oozing out
into the open.
It spilled out,
my pores glowing
with truth.
My jaw hung open
while silently,
and in full view
of everyone,
I gazed through
the thin fabric
of his white oxford
& thought lovingly
about his nipples.

8 MAY 2008 — ANCHORAGE, ALASKA

FIREWORKS

The fires had become hard to ignore, our skin sparking dangerously above the dry grass. There was always heat rising within me, and I was warming in the presence of bodies I felt so drawn to. I'd held too loosely, letting a Roman candle slip through my fingers as I thought about all the things I'd let slip through my fingers. And my friends had never considered how destructive I could be when I gave in and let the flames under my skin erupt to the surface. They tried to stomp it out, and I wondered when they'd come for all the other fires. We ran from the burning grass, but the smoldering continued wherever I went. For weeks, too afraid to know the extent of our destruction, we kept ourselves just inside the city. I kept fashioning increasingly elaborate and increasingly dangerous devices to let some of the fire out, otherwise I feared I might burst into flames and collapse in a pile of ashes in front of everyone. I hadn't realized yet that phoenixes like myself rise out of those ashes, so I remained afraid. For all I know, that field is still burning, twenty-five years later. The ashes are still smoldering, bursting back to life now and then.

28 MARCH 2008 — ANCHORAGE, ALASKA

Toll Collector
at the Barn

In darkness,
a blinding white light.

We were choking
on Bibles
& each other

so carefully
across the
limits of

acceptance

& your own
blooming into
a delicate magnolia.

16 JUNE 2021 — PAYNE COUNTY, OKLAHOMA

TRYST

Dry lips pressed
in January cold.
Hands on hands,
hands on shoulders,
hands on faces,
hands on backs,
hands wandering
the contours of budding muscles,
the lingering bony pubescence.
They touch together
peach-fuzzy faces,
blushed pink with youth,
erupting with passion,
with fear and confusion.
The taste of tongue
replaces every algebraic equation,
every chapter on natural selection,
every rehearsed Shakespearean line.
The two boys untangle at the bell,
the ringing forcing them
each to the dry loneliness
of their own mouths,
departing as strangers,
an invisible string
always tethering them
to these moments of exploration,
to awkward inexperience.

5 OCTOBER 1998 — CLAREMORE, OKLAHOMA

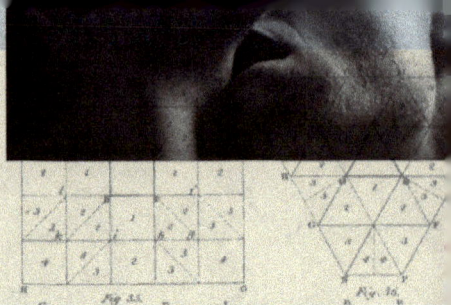

A BREATHLESS SOLITUDE

WITH ROBERT A. COZZI

"Come I will show thee shadows of the world
And images of life." [2]
                        — *Lord Alfred Douglas*

The permanence of love is barely dressed at dawn
The fleeting breaths at twilight glide together in ceremony
I'm focusing on the rhythm of tides, naked in moonlight
calculating rotations in hopes of harnessing the elusive sun
The coastline of my heart is warped and garish
As sweat tickles my sides and the sea echoes in the wind
Every finger seems to pull away, each lip just out of reach
Life flickers around me, an unwatched silent film
Achingly voiceless, the hush swallows me
Into the virgin expanse of uninvited solitude

2 JUNE 2021 — BASKING RIDGE, NEW JERSEY
PAYNE COUNTY, OKLAHOMA

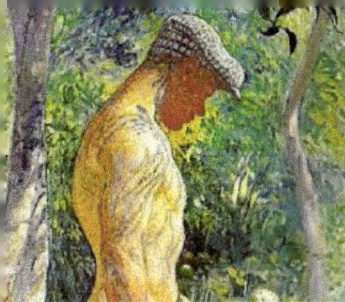

THE CRAFTING
OF WORDS REVEALS

"I am much too alone in this world, yet not alone
*   enough*
to truly consecrate the hour." [3]
                                    — *Rainer Maria Rilke*

A restless heart hangs on
Fear blocks its aching ventricles
Cracks in this old muscle become visible

Endless unspoken longings hang overhead
Screamed silently
The crafting of words reveals
Yearning
Unrequited and lonely

The last time you were here
I sang to you these songs
And in that moment
the breaking commenced

after Robert A. Cozzi, "The Stillness of Remembering"

11 JUNE 2021 — PAYNE COUNTY, OKLAHOMA

15

PARTLY CLOUDY

Now we discover ourselves
in quiet moments;
the skies blush in grey hues
& we are all connected to the
embarrassment of rain.

All of our children are marching,
performing for us in the safety of home.
Mine are still transparent; I look through
the spaces where I had meant to place them.
Sometimes I see these little faces
looking back at mine for approval.

Join me! Let's write our own fables.
We'll use our still-imagined children,
put them in danger,
let them get caught in storms.

for Emily Salt

8 AUGUST 2021 — PAYNE COUNTY, OKLAHOMA

Every Moon Hangs in the Night

I'm still waiting for the boys to make sense,
& you're at it again, slinking off to another
rendezvous with some guy whose name you
never bothered to ask.

I should be more surprised,
or maybe less shocked.

Every moon hangs in the night,
waiting to follow you home,
waiting to tell you stories.

I'm still waiting for these days to make sense,
& you're too busy running to notice,
too wrapped up—as you should be—in lusts,
in magnetism, in basic biology. In settling down,
like I should have done.

           It was always going to be me.

I should be more, or less,
whichever you'd prefer.
It isn't all lasagna & Plath anymore,
but I know I'd trade in all my lovers
for more of those hours

writing poetry at the truck stop.

for Jerry

22 JUNE 2021 — PAYNE COUNTY, OKLAHOMA

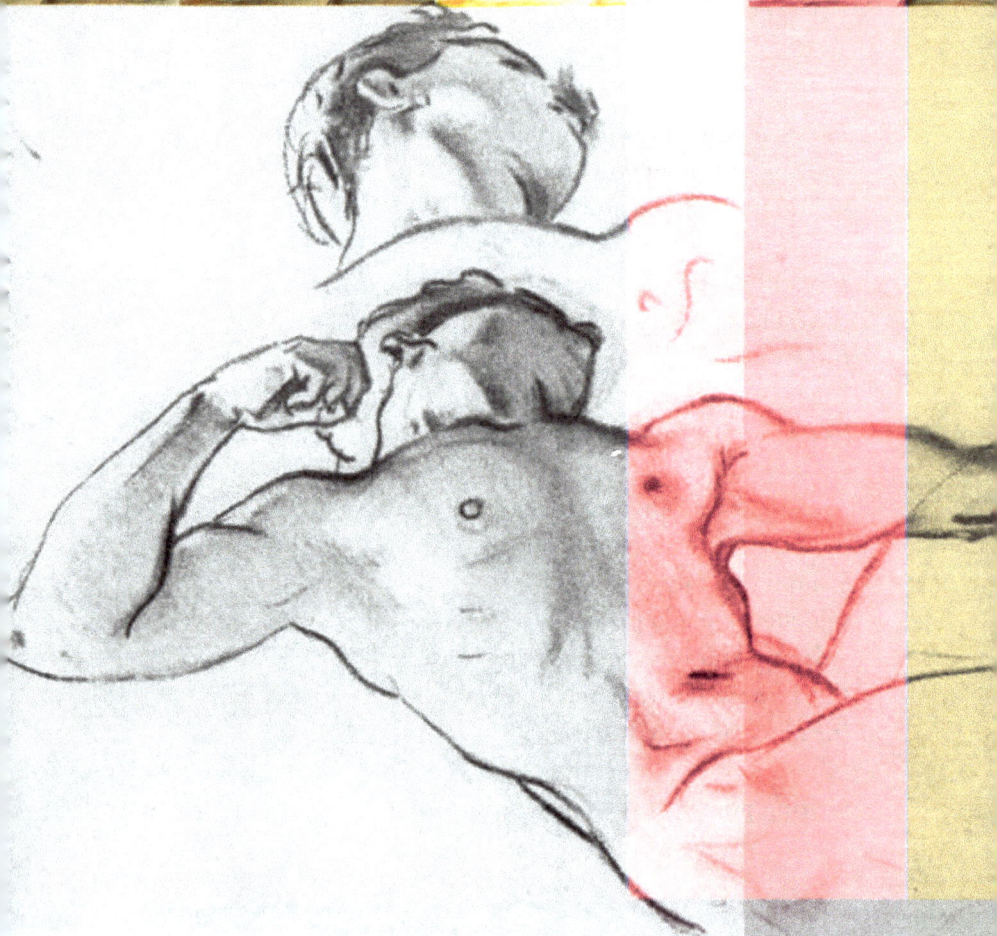

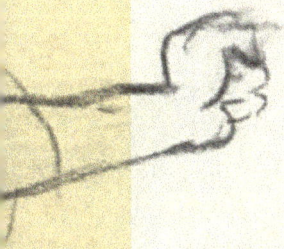

DUST

I'm gonna writhe around in the dusty road like a chinchilla until my skin feels like his skin, until my hair is rough and stained red, until I've learned to stop coughing out the earth from my lungs and start to become one with this place.

Box of Colors

17.

I built myself a box, brown-grey, lined in brilliant colors and patterns I thought others would never want to see, and I started my own years of judgment, mumbling about my life to people who never listened, smelling of malls and bookstores, of dusty old books I cherished and of dusty old books I clung to.
　　　　The sun would shine through the cracks,

　　　　　　　　lighting up the colors,
　　　　　　　　bursting and beautiful

　　　and I would dream about the joy I had been once,

　　　　　　　　about peach.

I felt rough and lonely, and I made effigies of those people I could have been from rocks, knickknacks, pieces of my friends. I looked into their crafted faces, and their eyes twinkled

　　　　　　　　like

　　　　　　stars.

Great cities seemed to sing songs to me, to lure me to the promise of orgies, of cold concrete, footsteps. I imagined myself there on their streets, as great men I was not, brilliant and full of patterns, the sun shining on my skin.

16 APRIL 2008 — ANCHORAGE, ALASKA
A VERSION ORIGINALLY APPEARED IN *SOCIAL DISTANCES* (2020)

THE FABRIC OF HIS SHIRT

I'm searching the fabric of his shirt,
    my hands sliding over the fibers,
    over seams and buttons, searching
    frantically for his naked body
    tangled in the folds of cotton.

What god is this, with so many hands
    pressing into my every places,
    surging with energy and anticipation,
    writhing so effortlessly around my creases?

We devour each other, two slender eels,
    sparking electricity from our slippery torsos,
    undulating & spinning over each other,
    desperate to become one.

The floor slams into us, and we barely notice
    as we shed jeans, most of our socks,
    first one sleeve of his shirt,
    then the other; mine is long since lost.
    Gasping, we acknowledge skin.

Thoughts turn to earlobes, which I pull
    gently with my teeth and my neck
    wets with his saliva. Eels.
    Everything is wet and urgent;
    I wince at the pain
    of needing to be inside him.

13 OCTOBER 2006 — ANCHORAGE, ALASKA

TIGERS

Maybe, just maybe I'm dancin'

like you said   I couldn't,
like you said   I wouldn't,
like you said   I mustn't,

You laughed in my face,
like my body was all dried up from the start,
like I'd been born without your human heart.
or maybe that little pebble in your head
forgot about my very humanness
just thought

nobody would dance with *that,*
slide across that sexless body
low —
        er themselves
        to that sad-faced
        pitiful creature.

Maybe, just — perhaps. Perchance,
        I've been dancin'
        all this time,

been so naked you'd gasp;
been so lewd you'd hide

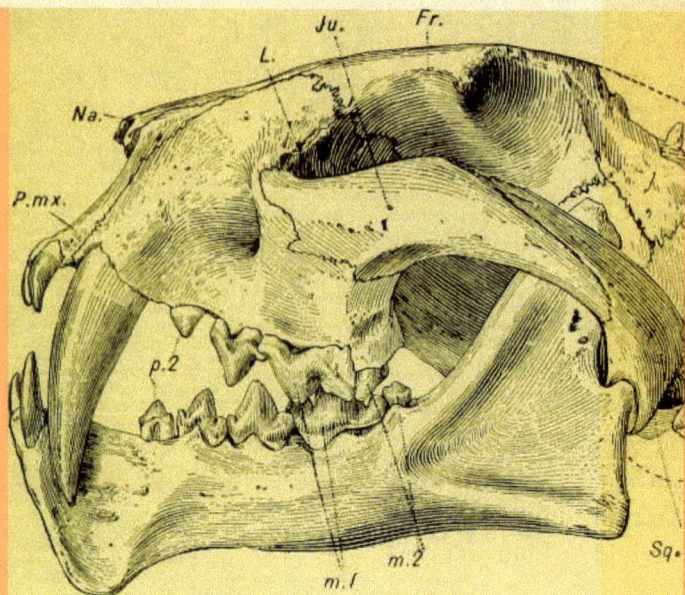

that hideous face
& run back to your mama.

There have been tigers,
        for sure,
great masses of fur and muscle,
teeth that tore into my tender flanks,
        ripped me
        free of this human body
        & split me open
                mid-pirouette.
I let them do it, wanted them to do it.

What? You thought I'd get all sad-faced again
& tear myself into tiny pieces,
        lonely as you

please,-d to mash the little
grey bits of dried tears
under my dance solos?

Um, no.

Yessir, there've been tigers,
but you wouldn't know about all that
& I'm not so sure your mama prepared you
to see the little hairs I plucked from their fur.

To see the teeth
left stuck in my ribs
during so much throbbing,
violent ecstasy.

So, if you don't
very much mind,
get your god-

damn hands off my neck

if you aren't going to choke me,
or fuck me,
or massage my throat
for the tiger songs
I learned in the burly arms of beasts.

Maybe, just maybe I'm dancin'

like *you*   couldn't,
like *you*   wouldn't,

like you said   I couldn't;
but   I would
&   I did.

APRIL 1999 — TULSA, OKLAHOMA
14 JUNE 2021 — PAYNE COUNTY, OKLAHOMA

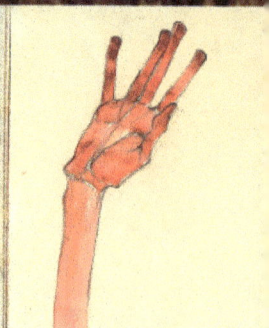

PIANO PLAYER AT THE GYPSY COFFEE HOUSE

He whispers a song to himself,
      over the sound of his own music,
      over the smell of roasted coffee,
      over the smoke of so many cigarettes.
I can taste each one — feel the pain in my own eyes
as the notes rise gently over the murmurs of intimate corners,
      poetry recited   impromptu
               stanzas swelling
               with Chopin's ghost
     and beyond a loosely hanging velvet curtain,
     accompanied by an off-key mandolin,
              strumming of a different song,
              a composition of its player,
              impromptu
              chords finding the rhythm
    the room pulling the thick air together,
    matching the stray piano notes.

Fingers — rough as the concrete
     of his workdays — stretch out
     across the slick warmth of piano keys.
          I imagine the fingers, closing my eyes

as though I need to memorialize,
as though I must dedicate my time
to future moments without the music
    impromptu
    pulling and pushing,
    pressing,
    caressing.

I'm staring at his lips, lost in the inaudible words,
    lyrics he must have written himself,
    not quite confident enough to vocalize,
    but his expression betrays him,
        and perhaps these words are spontaneous,
        whispered in the throes of my gaze.
            Is this all for me?
    This   impromptu concert
    is   more romantic
    than   rose petals pressed on skin.

He moves past Chopin, his unskilled Thelonious Monk
        melting my already heated soul
        and I become a shapeless mass,
        distant and fluctuating,
        taking on the form
    of   impromptu secrets.
The night rises, breaking out around the moon
through the stained glass windows
in the sprawling emptiness
of downtown.
We slide into
        impromptu tomorrows,
        wrapped in the poems and music
        and the last slice of chocolate cake.

14 JULY 2001 — TULSA, OKLAHOMA

AUSTIN, TEXAS

Heartbreak is a warm sensation
When the only feeling that you know is fear
                        —*Orville Peck*

The heat's been rising
waves scorching stripes into our sides
scorching across our memories
Youth evaporates so quickly
when you try to hold on

The gravitational pull of our loins
smoke and darkness—darkness
It's always been dark here
it's always been hot

Dance with me   in time with gravity
Dance with me   drunk on gin & beer
Dance with me   so we can just forget

Dance with me   so we can remember
Dance with   me

The fires are burning out of control
beyond our torn off shirts
chest hair & sweat gyrate to the music
but my ears have stopped working

Every thought I have ever conjured
escapes in the darkness
through the fog pumped in around
the gravitational forces

We exist   alone

Lick my lips. Lick my very soul in time to thuds
Thud—Thud—Thud—Tongue
I'm dreaming—I must be dreaming
but I'm never this drunk in my dreams
& my hands are never touching your chest
never damp with your sweat.

Kiss   me   without any hint of inhibition
Kiss   me   now as fully yourself
Kiss   me   so we will no longer be little boys
Kiss   me   so we will never forget
Kiss   me
                 so I can melt

                 into you

18 MARCH 2002 — AUSTIN, TEXAS

PLUTO PROJECTOR

Where's the dirty apartment I expected,
strewn with friends and strangers
all draped across each other?
My lap is always incomplete these days.

The film has faded.
I'm keeping the reels turning
so nothing else burns away,
melts into the voids
where I will eventually
find myself.

I want to press pause, pull everything out,
make a nest of my failures to sleep in.

Fuck the responsibilities of adulthood,
fuck the quiet,
and fuck whoever thought our lives
should be vacuumed free of the beautiful grit.

My eyes want to remain closed,
imagining the filth I deserve.
I'm so tired of the polished surfaces,
and my pristine liver.

My scratches are artificial,
fraudulent lives I've invented
for the interest of strangers.
They'll never know about the quiet days
when I just sit happily,
reliving how fortunate (blessed, as they say)
my life has been.
That will never do.

I see so many husband-shaped spaces,
they are all I see when I'm not drowning
in the ridiculousness of joy.

I'm still waiting.

inspired by the Rex Orange County song

25 MARCH 2021 — PAYNE COUNTY, OKLAHOMA

NECTAR

WITH JUSTIN WARD

My wings are etched maps,
      directions to you,
      to elusive blooming,
      to unfurling petals,
      to the sweet reward of my chrysaloid patience.

How sweet, how good, how seductive you've grown.

You blush
      in colors never seen before,
      in reds and blues,
      the greens of your youth,
      in blindingly brilliant pinks and yellows.

      Open for me,
      let me suckle on your sweetness,
      lap my tongue around your pistil
as you caress me with the tips
of flamboyant, dancing stamens.

6 JUNE 2015 & 9 JUNE 2021 — PAYNE COUNTY, OKLAHOMA

Your Beauty in February

Dear handsome creature, teach me
  how to be beautiful,
  how to fuck and love
  someone so smooth-skinned
  & perfectly formed — otherworldly.
  Your lips are soft petals & strong;
  press them into me everywhere.
Overwhelm my kisses & attempts
to make you stay forever.

Let's shape the universe into a nest
where we can watch everything
drift apart until nothing is left.
But the very limit of time
is not nearly long enough.

19 FEBRUARY 2002 — TULSA, OKLAHOMA

35

YOUR BEAUTY IN APRIL

Dear sweet honeysuckle,   so young & Polish.
                          It must end.
               Your kisses flatter me,
                & these strokes through your hair,
           or mine; nibbles of fingers.
           I long to touch every contour,
       every gentle sloping guide
      to the places where I'd kiss you forever.
Your pillowy moans haunt me,
distract me in unexpected moments,

& I start contorting, absentmindedly
mimicking my favorite positions.

Dear sweet, delicious god,   I want to watch you forever,
                      your face in rapturous throes
             of gentle thrusts,
             the world melting away,
          leaving only your body & mine,
          locked in lovemaking.
       I don't want everything to return,
      or anything at all beyond this now.
When time parts us, as time will part us all,
keep my name on your lips. Always

whisper to me in your own language,
in the stillness of your own solitude.

17 APRIL 2008 — ANCHORAGE, ALASKA

WHITE

WITH CHERYL COUTURE

I'm opening   to possibilities,
           to gods who will turn my spent body
           into the most beautiful flowers
              you've never seen.
I'm opening   to the spreading of your legs,
           to the great burst of light as I climax & see the
divinity of every atom from myself to the very edges of space. In
that moment, time and space split—you might call it heaven, or
nirvana, or the pure simplicity of the present and the collision of
our bodies. The electrostatic I see when I close my eyes too
fast.

      Bright white
      like the softest part of my tummy;
      like the unused tissue at my grandmother's funeral;
      like the last bit of light under heavy eyelids before going
under, so a surgeon can cut into my body;
      like a flake of ejaculate on my new velvet headboard.
      like the sensation of falling through nothing;
      like a choir of angels smiling silently as Apollo takes my
hand & leads me to his bed.

27 MARCH 2008 — ANCHORAGE, ALASKA
24 AUGUST 2020 — AUSTIN, TEXAS

THE NEXT MORNING

Before you go,
give me your contact info;
let me slip into all of your DMs.
Touch my arm—press memories into my pores.
The days of waiting will feel too long,
already feel too long as I let your fingers escape,
cement myself here where I expect you to see
every thought of abandonment and longing,
the image I'm pausing of your body
silhouetted in the doorway
when you must have thought I was sleeping.

Time is slipping away from me.

The sun is so warm.
I'm spending most of my morning
letting the hairs of my chest
remain matted together

just in case I never see you again.

My bed is already growing,
the emptiness announcing itself in uncomfortable silence.
I'm trapped in this loveless marriage with absence,
with the you-shaped space that holds my attention.
I feel the universe expand around me.

25 MARCH 2021 — PAYNE COUNTY, OKLAHOMA

INSTAGRAM

How many thoughts can I write,
stuffed neatly into square boxes?

Your magic, it touches me,
that flower is pretty and so are you,
that flower is lovely like your soul,
your eyes are filled with the dew of a thousand roses in May…

I've already gone too far,
written more words than you'll read.
I'm trying to make this short,
to get right to the point
before you get bored and move on,
but I can't cut out this part… it's too important.

My hair is distracting me,
still long from quarantine,
getting longer because everyone is still covered in viruses.
But I'm trying to make this brief,
looking for the vocabulary to make succinct points.
Where are you in such a hurry to go?
I thought we were all stuck at home
watching endless hours of baking competitions,
groggily refusing to turn off slow movies,
discovering new iterations of burritos, cakes,
testing everything in the air fryer.
I know, I know, I'm still going on about this.

> *You are as beautiful as a sunset*
> *and I am so deeply sad and withered inside….*
which words did you want me to use?
What cliché would make you happiest?
> *A thousand tiny horses have kissed my forehead,*
> *and they remind me of how much you mean to me…*
That doesn't even mean anything,
but would you like me to put it in bold text on a poster?

How many words do I have left to write?

17 OCTOBER 2020 — PAYNE COUNTY, OKLAHOMA

HOW MUCH TIME DID YOUR CREATION TAKE [5]

Dance, when you're broken open
Dance, if you've torn the bandage off.
Dance in the middle of the fighting.
Dance in your blood.
Dance, when you're perfectly free. [6]
—*Rumi*

O angel of Angels

Apollo is weeping alone in his Amyclaean temple;
the sweet sugar of young beauty drained from the nectar
of his most beautiful flower, now withered and limp,
soaked in its own blood and in the soil of its ancestors.
New blooms are already forming by the power of grief,
but their petals cannot compare to what has been lost.

O angel of Cyparissus

Pan has retreated to solitude in the forest of the Zagros.
He is mourning as he had mourned for Daphnis.
His flute's music moves through the branches of oak trees,
hauntingly filling the rocky slopes where the leopards hide.
All joy has slipped back to heaven, to Hermes' broken heart.
There is no longer any purpose in dancing.

O angel of Yazata

The twisting began as humans took our first breath,
arrogance settling in before humility ever stood a chance.
As a flower, you were always too beautiful for safety.
The grasses and trees delight in their jealousy;
they excluded the flowers from their mythical stories,
foolishly insist in their own sacredness, ignoring the gods.

O angel of Daniel

How could you have known that you were among lions?
How could you have known of your missing wings?
The lions salivated with lusts of their own, blood and power,
raised you so carefully for sacrifices to their emptiness.
The ground bones, centuries of ancestors, shift the earth,
the undiscovered artifacts shattering in grief.

O angel of Ātar

It's far too sad to consider all the blooming you had done,
and far too important to ignore the fires started by loss,
by the infinite joys you've missed, by the need to dance.
You're free now, angel, liberated sadly by the devouring.
Your wings have been returned; your skin glows radiantly.
Rise now to heaven, to dance, and to light the world on fire.

صدای گریه ی ابری [7]

in memory of Alireza Fazeli-Monfared
27 MAY 2021 — PAYNE COUNTY, OKLAHOMA

PEN-D-ULES

swing
& I'm mil-
ling
about
in front of
my temp (les)(ests)(os),

/
tick
\
tick
/
tick
\
tick

,dwelling   in

       pain that never
numbs.

Waiting

for others
       to dismantle e.v.e.r.y.t.h.i.n.g.
allatonceblastthroughthewallsi'vebuilt
inburstoftheshrapneloflies&memories&
dirtylittlesecretswecannevertell.

Still— tick   tick   tick   tick
& I'll just blow
it all   up my
self.

there's been too much
wa—

       —it—

           —in—

              —g.

The numbing
will come

after   de   str   uct   ion

after

it all.

I crave
the

*tick

      tick
tick
      tick*

numb
ing.

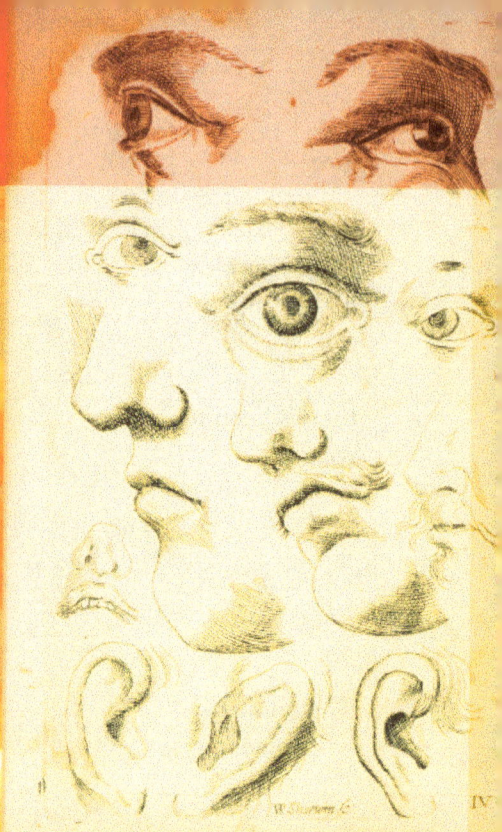

Naked Bodies

If you'd only understood what I meant,
how deeply I wished to taste your neck.

If I had arrived svelte as my Irish ancestors,
would you have lost your inhibitions and fucked me madly?

If I had arrived rugged as a German millworker,
the edges of my clothes still damp from work,
would you have forgotten yourself and fallen into my arms?

Your very being is what most turns me on about you,
when I'm alone and start to think about how I missed my
opportunity to be with you or to be you.

I was never very adept at being myself, and I think you knew,
hated that,   hated me.

If I could've had just 15 minutes with you, you'd have
understood everything I have yet to become and just how
perfect I could be for any of your 15 minutes.

If I could've had just an afternoon with you, you'd be married
by now, but not necessarily to me.

I'm learning Czech because I want to sleep with you.

I'm learning Castilian because I want to sleep with you.

I'm learning French because I want to touch you.

I'm learning German because I don't always know who I am.

I'm learning imaginary languages because I try too hard.

I want to show you every hidden tattoo while we dissect the
understandings of selves and the soils we feel between our
toes.

I've found the perfect thing to eat off your body. I'm
practicing on my own thighs, imagining my fingers as yours?

I'll never stop thinking about your contours.

11 NOVEMBER 2011 — ANCHORAGE, ALASKA

49

LES SOUVENIRS
DE PETIT GARÇON

My own collections
overflowed with
    innocence,
    ignorance
dreams of the sea, secrets told on the wizened bodies of
pufferfish & seahorses, dust collecting on translucent skin.

My joys were found in scallop pink hues
& the rattling of soft white sand dollars,

still pregnant with secret angels
    or doves.

I've forgotten which I was told by the merfolk whispering from
the depths of the queen conch that spent its time on Mom's sink,
along with her many bottles of mysteries that smelled so
strange.

Mom collected that shell as a girl, on vacation in Texas.
    I had never been to the ocean, never looked out across
for a glimpse of Poseidon on the blue horizon.

We were still living in our little boy bodies, barely making sense of clothes that always closed around us like those shells, barely making sense of the sounds we heard in everything, our little ears pressed against them, imagining the crashing of waves.
He had pulled off his pants,
his parents having instructing us
to bed.
He wanted to show me the things he had collected, the things he wanted to show his friend. So, he pressed his baby body into my back, still clothed, and told me things he shouldn't know.

It's fun to share,
shells,
stories,
experiences.

Time pushed us apart

—too far apart—

& my eyes are shut fast.
I'm humming to myself
& I wonder if he heard the merfolk
singing through the emptiness,
heard the crashing of the waves,

understood
innocence.

inspired by the François Raoult song
25 MARCH 2021 — PAYNE COUNTY, OKLAHOMA

PENANCE FOR MY CRIMES

Forgive these unsettled roots,
this aged and rough bark,
and this (deeply bloodstained)
javelin, taken from the deer's
lifeless body,
punched here in my side
at just where your handprint
has not yet faded.
Some days I'm too tired
to hold out my arms
while the birds
rear their chicks in my elbows.
and I can't stop noticing
the absence of fingers
pulling me close,
the knots forming
where memories of our bonded
flesh burns too hot
for my budding green leaves.

30 MAY 2021 — PAYNE COUNTY, OKLAHOMA

PHANTOM

My heart is clutched
phantom hands
reaching through tissues
sliding through fingers
I wither in a heap,
cold and weak,
death drawing
closer than my breaths.
I cannot make out
the phantom's form
& I fear that it is me.

25 JULY 2004 — TULSA, OKLAHOMA

A Confession

What makes me a fraud
is the clarity of the film
when I play it back.
Sure, it's burned in a few places
where I'd stop the projector too long,
let the heat obscure reality until it was gone,
the stories now written down fictions
of a life I intended to live.
Those spots look like experience,
fooling others who think I've lived as fully,
unaware of the agony of waiting,
the slow rotation of a full year
when I just stand still and watch the sun
as we encircle and spin.

What makes me a fraud
is the excuses I've built around myself,
the libraries I've filled with comparisons
to my friends' lives, so richly lived,
the lives I tell myself I must have lived
and which I failed to understand.

25 MARCH 2021 — PAYNE COUNTY, OKLAHOMA

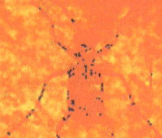

TURTLES ALL THE WAY DOWN

Let's just be honest,
this is taking far too long.
Memories of me will fail
to understand the extent
of all the failures.

I've missed far too much;
I'm trying to pry open
the universe itself, crawl
into the opening. I
don't care what I find there.

Nothing looks right now;
the dreams are scorched in places,
those moments when I stood still,
let true purity destroy
everything that should be.

If you're wondering,
I've wrapped myself in warm dreams,
let naïve lies comfort my brain,
gave them importance
I reserved for myself.

inspired by the Sturgill Simpson song
25 MARCH 2021 — PAYNE COUNTY, OKLAHOMA

BEFORE I DROWN

I'm so landlocked that the clouds have gathered bits of oceans to bring as a gift to lay at my still-dry feet, to give me a spot to drown in the same water we used to nourish the roses, the same water of our mothers' tears, and the same dripping water of ancient glaciers that formed before our oldest ancestors first climbed down from the trees and felt their dry feet on the land. I'm admonishing myself for admonishing myself, chastising myself for chastising myself, Danny's right words going

through my head, Danny Wright's words lifting me up, Danny's write words opening up my mind and reaching across the ocean to let me know that others appreciate me, appreciate words, appreciate the small intricacies that draw me into my own alienation. His words flash new worlds in my mind, they are touching my tongue that no longer tries do devour its host, tamed into sweetness, tamed into only searching for mouths to kiss. They are spraying on my skin like the waters encircling pulling us north from Devon, further north from Arranmore, the drops darkening into memories of immigrant ancestors who never really left the comfort of their island homes. They kept it with them, speckled along their arms and legs as souvenirs, memories. The spots have stayed with me as well, reminded me to look across the water, reminded me to stay connected to it. These moments don't last long enough, as the drops gather, and soon only echoes of poets I had once read drift into the distance until I dare to let them in again. The pipes, the pipes are fading. Still, the clouds keep delivering these drops that are so familiar. Maybe someday I'll step my foot on my ancestors' homeland, feel the familiarity of the native grasses in my toes. Maybe I'll drown before then, reading through my library of books as the waters rise. But I have to remember to not apologize for being so great, to not feign coyness for everything I've built from these handed down stories, my own words, my words that I hope cross oceans and project memories in other people's minds.

for D.B. Wright

23 AUGUST 2021 — PAYNE COUNTY, OKLAHOMA
ORIGINALLY APPEARED IN *SCISSORTAIL QUARTERLY* #4 (AUGUST 2021)

59

fag(got

youreal mad,
babycakes &
it ain't my   pro-blem
your   mama mess
                ed you all up.
so, we gonna make
out, or you
gon
        jus
                stan
                    ther
                        slac
                            jawd
                            caus
                            i sparkl?

i'd prol hate me too   seein how mag   ickle, i.
                            how god
                            damn fab
                            u
                            lous
                            hvn all these rain
                            beaus
                            fallin
                            from my fingers.

fuck it,
jus kis s s s s s
me already.
i won't tell,   les you want me to.

you don't
think   i'm still   !!!

ohbabycakes,
i'm getting my face kicked in
on no

s.I'd.walk.

                    we rad-
                    iate
                    now.

          git into it.

20 AUGUST 1998 — CLAREMORE, OKLAHOMA
5 JUNE 2021 — PAYNE COUNTY, OKLAHOMA

THE SNOW IN HER EYES

27.

A great man once told me that everything in the future was to be a steady decline downhill. It was my twenty-seventh birthday. I had reached my peak, my summit. Nothing would ever be as good as it had been.

His breath smelled of lavender, and I never stopped wanting to see his body. But his words haunted me. They still do, even though he would go on to meet a woman to marry and he would father beautiful children with her. Apparently, it isn't necessarily all downhill. I was transforming myself into a person I couldn't recognize and his words stuck in my own throat as if I had been the one who spoke them.

I had become a vile sycophant,
   prostrating myself before pretend-friends,
   before those who enjoyed and demanded my groveling and praise.

They never knew how much I knew.

They never understood that I was aware of how little they thought of me. I prostrated myself, not because they deserved to be idolized, but because I deserved to grovel.

I had once seen snow falling
   in my grandma's eyes.

I had gone to Alaska to find that snow, to uncover the reasons it had stayed in her eyes, to understand why she had let me dance in her peach nightgown in spite of her firm grip on expression. I had gone to find Dad, to find his dad, to find myself a man of my own to grow old and grey with.

> I was just a swishy little boy
> head full of promises and lies.

Had she let me see the snow
        or did I see what she tried to hide?

This wasn't a place where I could find anyone; it was a place where men had climbed mountains to place an electric-lit star, a memorial to a Middle Eastern dissident they pretended to understand. But they weren't overturning tables and embracing radical love. A rebellious young man, a man who dared to say that those who live on society's edges deserve respect, was now being worship as the god of selfishness and greed. The god of moral failings, of inadequacies, of stupidity, of White Supremacy, of the guns they jerk off and jerk off to.

I was not where I meant to be.

> I was looking for chiffon.

> The mountains ripped open the skies,
> snow falling from the green ribbons.

That ostentatious star was more or less ignored on those cold days, but I am still thinking about it now and wondering if I am still that ugly man trying so hard to make people love him.

16 APRIL 2008 — ANCHORAGE, ALASKA
A VERSION ORIGINALLY APPEARED IN *SOCIAL DISTANCES* (2020)

ANNEMARIE IS DOING
HER LAUNDRY

It's such a lovely afternoon for this everything,
      for these folks who hang their lives onto lines
      of poetry, emotions—wet
      & newly washed—pain.
      My metaphors keep me distant, cloud-bound
         & deep in stories I'm trying to tell.
      I'm passing through; reality is never as nice
      as one might have hoped in dreams about it.
         And the dreams are never as nice
      as one might have hoped in the wide-eyed
      awareness of reality.
Jairo is inventing words again,
      forgetting himself on the edges
      & stepping one foot in front of the other
      like he learned as a good little Mormon boy
      in his pressed white oxford,
      but now he's reversing it all,
      never watching where he's going
      and in the end it all just works out the same,
      just like it did for other former Mormons, friends,
         when they matured past it all.
      I think a lot about how much we never discussed,
      & who they must believe that I am. They're wrong,
         I'd imagine, but who can say for sure.
I am focused on writing cantos for chattering squirrels,
      love sonnets for wayward raccoons,

but that all feels too silly when I think about it,
far too loudly and I hear the leg of Robert's chair
scrape its horrible noise across the floor
which wakes me from daydreams
& reminded me that there is more to life
                than beauty.
At this moment, I remember my own name
being spoken, but I've been too far gone,
and I never did try to discover where I had been
or why they had invoked my name.
Sometimes, I get so tired I can barely hold
        my eyes open, and I slump
        sideways,   reaching down to the floor
        like I'm performing an elaborate ballet,
        still sat in my chair,
        & I chase the words around my screen,
                so many little boxes and they all squish
        together into an impressive piece of
        brutalist architecture.
                I yawn — pandiculate over-dramatically
        — spittle flying out across onto the corner
        of my computer's screen,
        And then I rise up, majestically,
        my exhaustion at last conquered by my dance.
        I triumphantly shake my mane,
        & resume my writing,
        slightly renewed.
Robert is chuckling at nothing — well I say
        nothing — he's found an amusing thought
        left to wander about in his brain
        for these many hours.
        He's not wearing his glasses (as he should),
        but it's not all that late — my own dramatics

& choreography notwithstanding.
We all wish he'd wear his glasses,
but Robert's making assurances
        I don't believe.
It's a steady in and out of recitations,
        strummed guitars—which I love
        more than I had ever loved—and
        plugging of books we are all so eager to read.
        I think a lot of Emily, and think she should
        always be around, but she has a family,
        which I also think is such a lovely thing to have,
                and which I do not have.
I'm lurking again, typing out my words
        over the clamor of their discussions,
        & it's almost like it had been before,
        when Jerry and Jennie were around,
        and we'd read to each other Sylvia Plath,
        Adrienne Rich, and Frank O'Hara.
        As it often does, the topic changes to hot dogs,
        or to the beautiful deli sandwiches
        enjoyed by carpenters in New York,
        or to the accidental succulence of a ripe peach,
                and I chuckle   because it's all so
                suggestive and unsubtle,
                and still they somehow fail to realize
                the sex dripping from their very words.
        Here, the universe is settled and sure of its own self.
        This now bloats with eternities,
                extensions of selves—our-,
                but never exclusively—
                in quiet crafting of everythings, possibility
        is possible.

11 JUNE 2021 — PAYNE COUNTY, OKLAHOMA

For Robert Q. Lewis

The New York lights
through precocious smoke,
scatter over the ghosts of my awakenings,
lost secrets in neatly pressed liaisons.
We have been your Mansfield Theatre
from the moment we stood upright,
and we've threaded your stories
through time, laughing as
you hid us away in your shadows
to raise the children you never could.
Listen to the chirping crickets
singing the songs we taught them.
Listen as we fill the shadows with joy.

Lavender little crickets
in lavender little shadows.

Lavender little lies
engulfed in lavender laughter.

20 JANUARY 2020 — PAYNE COUNTY, OKLAHOMA

CHRISTMAS BLUE

I still hear your voice,
your pet names & affirmations.
I feel your breath on my neck,
the remainders of Zephyrus
still clinging to your lungs
in slow, warm puffs, in moist
& soothing sighs.

Your skin was so smooth
that night—like satin, like velvet.

It it occurs to me now that the rug
where we spent draped over each other
was so richly blue, saturated,
a blue that reminds me of Christmas
cards, of men on camel back
framed in silver like the moon
on your face in the night
as I watched you sleep.

I feel the color so deeply,
now that I'm left here alone.
Everything shines so yellow
in the absence of the moon.
Return to me and ignite
the blue again.

4 JANUARY 2000 — TULSA, OKLAHOMA

HONEYSUCKLE

Soft yellow
petaled cloud dragon,
botanical zodiac myth,
wise and ancient flower,
     consummate your
     hummingbird love affair,

tongues intertwining
in pools of nectar,
in leafy green mists,
in vining corded masses.
They cling to everything.

The flames of your breath
bleach white in the sun,
& I pull the strings
to cool my tongue's tip
with your sweet sugar.

These summer days are
so hot and moist,
the days are engulfed
in rising passions.
     Only fire-bodied lovers
     venture into daylight.

for Justin

7 JUNE 2021 — PAYNE COUNTY, OKLAHOMA

DANIEL, ON HIS BIRTHDAY

To be an artist and troubled
untroubled and beautiful
beautiful as you are and…

My dreams are more vivid than the used to be
and I can't figure out how you've done that.
Maybe it's something in the pigments you used,
maybe it's something in the pigments of your eyes.

Everything reminds me of you
reminds me of laughter,
reminds me to stop and take notice

The squirrels are chattering,
chasing each other across the fallen trees,
flirting, as they do, in spirals up the trunks
of pecans festooned with Virginia creeper.

You were looking back at me through
the ceramic eyes of that white stag.
You're in everything
I wonder if you're real, if you…

I'm whispering secrets about you
to myself on cold nights. I'm wondering
what you're creating — love, beauty,
magic, great   catastrophes,   or…?

I wonder what your tattooed skin feels like.
Your hands. I'm in love with who
I am when I think about you.

15 JANUARY 2010 — ANCHORAGE, ALASKA

IMMORTALITY

I've just read a poem by Paul Lorenz. Jesus! There's so much left for me to learn. The cats are restless tonight. They must know how important everything feels to me right now. I'm so worried about my dead friends, and about all the friends who have not died, but still I never see them anymore. I thought we said we wouldn't do that to each other. Maybe we expect too much of the dead, keeping the insignificant bits of them with us—trash really, or at least things that if donated would be of use to someone, use beyond the reminder that too many are no longer here.

The artist who rendered this painting got my proportions all wrong, and maybe I should ask him to try again, but this time make me taller. Or maybe I have no business telling the artist what I look like. They can see *me*! Far more clearly than I can see myself.

I want to know everything.

My mind is shredded, beautiful images of people I shouldn't think about; people who so often can't even see me standing here, and not just because I appear in proportions closer to how that artist had seen me.

Someday, a poet will write lines about me, a whole poem perhaps, & that day can't come too soon. I want to be immortalized, fallen in love with, & live forever in those lines.

6 JUNE 2002 *&* 11 MARCH 2003 — TULSA, OKLAHOMA

PROFFERS THE MEANING
OF THE STARS [8]

Remember when the world was warm and clear, [9]
and you're sure to be happy with the results. [10]

I am the stars the moon the planets; [11]
I was young enough to kill myself for art, [12]
too intricate and transitory to pin down, [13]
"I guess that's why we like him." [14]

How can this be the same sun? [15]
If the moon smiled, she would resemble you… [16]

I'm so tired of chasing the illusion of a life with no
consequences. [17]
You cannot kill a poet or a poem! [18]

There are dead people all around us: [19]
a collection of perfect specimens [20]
as phantom after-image. [21]
I envied them the elegance of their ease [22]
when the stars threw down their spears. [23]

a cento remnant for lost friends
28 MARCH 2021 — PAYNE COUNTY, OKLAHOMA

EXTINCTION

The vapors of my breaths are exquisitely rare; collect and display them behind glass before it's too late and memory of me slips into history. Everything should go on display. Will you include the frogs found stuck in my throat? They've kept my lungs closed, hardening off slowly with an ever fading supply of oxygen. My youth had once spilled out with endless possibility, but maybe it had been too much and too quickly I found myself trudging though a thickness that I mistook for fog. It was the dissolution of everything I was meant to be, growing and thickening with every passing year, every passing day, every passing hour, minute, second... What parts will be important enough for the Earth to fossilize them? None? What if there is nothing worth preserving and my memory is best left in the moments when my lungs took in the air around me, burned the fires of my ancestors deep in my heart? My memories won't all go on without me, my resentments will die where they expanded, my joys will fail to light up a world that so often needs the additional light. Will you display the light of my soul in a museum with my femur and skull?

How do you know who you are? No, really, I'm asking. How do you know? I keep dancing inside. Is that how you knew you were when you first figured that out? How do you know you are beautiful? I only know that I'm traveling this life in an exoskeleton that isn't always shaped like others want. I only know that I'm traveling this life in a cloak of flesh that makes it so hard to fall in love with me superficially. I've always wanted to be loved superficially, to be lusted after and desired… touched roughly. There have been too many…too many…too many… Boys who didn't find what they wanted, men who looked through me and didn't want to see beyond, friends who made assumptions. Boys who couldn't look up at me when I greeted them good morning because they had no time for unattractive people.

Attractive? Attractive, beautiful, lovely, desirable, sexy, alluring, enchanting, hot, manly, rugged, gorgeous, hollow, vapid, delightfully empty. I've found myself in men's bedrooms, curled on the floor as far away from them as I could get. I wouldn't want to have any of this fleshy form stain the beauty of taut skin, the definition of muscles. I've woken up in men's bedrooms, draped on chairs. My cells sloughed off and I silently prayed he wouldn't see me, and that he would allow me to slip back to my life. There have been so many parts that have never quite fit, pushed in awkwardly or jutting out, slipping over in places where other men have the marks where the gods sculpted them. I've never been loved by Hephaestus; I was an experiment of sorts, in soft clay and the tissues of dead animals. He did fill me with a fire, as he likes to do, and I've found that fire a comfort at times when my house grows cold from years of emptiness.

I'm tagging my parts, taking control of the narrative of my memory, as if I have any right to manipulate my history. Who am I to decide my own legacy, to erase the older men who only pretended to understand me? I'm more chiseled than you'd ever understand, more ruggedly handsome than you can see in photos, or reconstruct from my remains. I'd recommend starting with the remains, as fresh as you can. It's my skin that

is so distracting, so repellant. Most of the boys didn't bother to be honest about that, but I could always see myself reflected in their beautifully moisturized faces.

Preserve my cells. Celebrate my mitochondria. It's so beautiful. It deserves a exhibition of its own, a museum dedicated to the full story of its possibility and the secrets it reveals about the universe, about sex, about the nature of what we so often refer to as god. How do you know who you are? So often, I find myself dancing with god, swirling stardust settling over and over across this insignificant lump that slowly became aware of itself. God lives in my reticula, closes his eyes around my membranes, merges his atoms with mine. At times, I transform into new elements, beyond the human understanding of chemistry. I dance as dissipated as quarks, so many multitudes of myself it's nearly impossible to understand the universe in my presence. And so, preserve this all. It's too beautiful to live in the past with my face's form.

What do I make of the vapor of my breath? Every beautiful thing has passed through me, passed through every leaf of every tree. I've touched every grain of sand and every speck of dust. They have been a part of my skeleton and my lips, and this body those men didn't want.

How do you know who you are? I am god.

8 JUNE 2021 — PAYNE COUNTY, OKLAHOMA

My First

My mythologies
crumbled as
we touched

FRAGMENTS IN THE RAIN

WITH MAX ASBEEK BRUSSE AND JARROD HOL

There's magic in tonight's laziness,
in the calm of a city warm with rain.
My cynicism is slipping away,
in this cleansing shower
and for a moment peace flows through me.
Puddles smile back at me,
street lanterns light the way as I am lost in thought.
Raindrops tick on the cars like a constant hi-hat,
tss.tss.tss.

I imagine this band of nature
jamming on the symphony of circumstance.
I'm so lost in thought, I don't notice
your ghost creeping up behind me.
I miss when I couldn't tell
where my hair was ending
and yours was beginning.
I miss when I couldn't tell
where my breath was ending
and yours was beginning.
I miss when we'd walk home
on rainy days, clothes soaked through
and we'd spend hours letting everything dry
under the radiant starry sky.
I miss everything we were
and all that we were never.
Everything has probably been said before
a million times,
a million different ways,
but I don't care; it's true.
The rain patters away,
tss.tss.tss.
I continue on, lost in the memory of us
wringing my brain, releasing the tears of the past.
And each step becomes a little lighter.

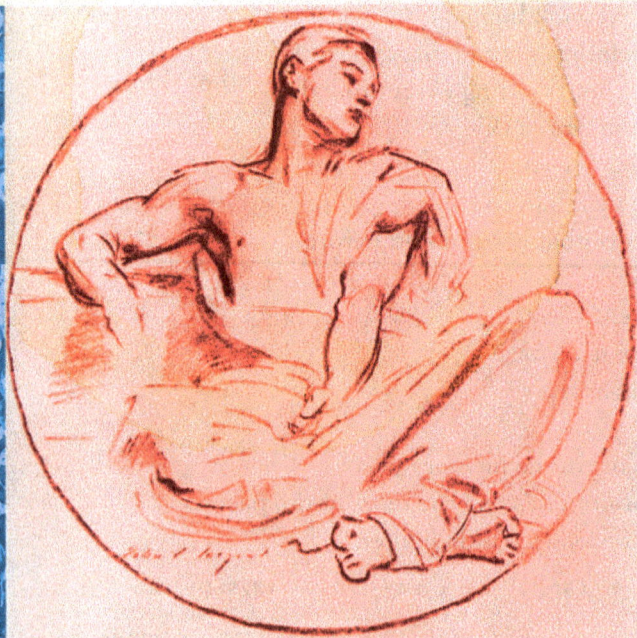

REQUIEM FOR MYSELF

1.
I want something tattooed on my arm, as beautiful as the park full of young men in mid-June, & I want a joint.

There were such beautiful flowers when I was young, but they're tied now to that fleeting youth. Today's blooms desaturate themselves, never even bothering to bloom in their fullness for me.

Let's go down to the park today, to admire the flowers and the men—this year's new geese waddling across the footpaths. I'm so eager to feel the warm breeze and hear the clamor of Summertime.

2.
I want you to see me here, imagine my tongue—my fingers. I want to lose myself in floating, out and above myself through time and space—beyond the icy blue pensiveness of Uranus, beyond the deep blue loneliness of Neptune.

Let me kiss you, my hands holding the square-beauty of your jaw that I first admired through the window of that Tulsa bookstore. Lets lie in bed on lazy Summer afternoons & let the sunlight blind us through the curtains.

Alone, I sunbathe out front, the green porch swing a perfect spot for napping, and I think of every beautiful thing while the sun beats down on my face. I'm still not sure I quite love that star, but we keep trying, keeping each other company in your absence.

3.

I want the trees to forgive me for pissing between them, too drunk to ask permission, too giddy with anticipation to care. I want you to leave me notes to find on mornings when you let me sleep in, and keep bringing me snacks you thought were my favorite, even though it isn't true. I don't want to correct you; the lighting up of your face is far too adorable.

Do you think we should put in roses along the back? I think we should put in roses. They remind me of everyone who should still be here, but so beautiful and fragrant.

4.

I want a half-erect penis, pulled from the stranger's jeans in a department store restroom. I knew he'd be there, in spite of my coyness, but I only looked, admiringly, too afraid to allow myself an inhibition. My mother was waiting beyond the door.

I want to feel alive, to live in distant memories of things I could never find. I want people to see the me I am in the solitude of home, the me I erupt into & who never seems to hold onto to the touch of another man.

My past is starting to pile up with mistakes, and none are the mistakes I thought I was making. If we reset everything, I'd find myself in far more strangers' homes than I have. I want to feel new hands on my shoulders, on my thighs.

5.
I want you to kill me—if the mood strikes you—but only if you tenderly touch me first. That might be enough. That might be the same as living, if only for a moment. Shove the javelin deep inside until I can no longer make a sound.

I want my heart broken, slumped despairingly in bed. At least that would mean I'd shared your company. At least I would have know that I was alive.

6.
I want to return triumphantly, to the place where I knew rejection so acutely. I'd burst in—mid-sermon—and... just stand there, I suppose. There are far too few who took any interest in where my life had taken me, and far too few left alive who I care to know. Some things are better in the past.

The planets all look the same from here, under the stars. I'm more lonely than I've ever felt before. That hasn't been enough.

7.
I want to experience the divinity of the universe, to be overcome with joy and madness during sex or to have my body's remains spread over the places I love the most, feeding the soils there.

You are my religion! Your chest a temple, your feet the ground on which I worship. When I look into your eyes, I know the truth of everything. Wrap me in the poems of your sacred text.

1997-2021 — OKLAHOMA, ALASKA & TEXAS

MOONLIGHT DISTRACTIONS

I'm watching the fluttering reflections,
fireflies drifting above rain puddles,
stars on a clear night far from the city's lights,
spots on a young fawn hiding
in the dappled sun at the forest's edge,
freckles on my pale skin,
which ignite with accidental touches.

I miss the sound of your breath
when you've stopped yourself saying
the things we were both thinking,
the feeling of soft lips kneading
each other in the glow of moonlight.

31 MAY 2021 — PAYNE COUNTY, OKLAHOMA

AURAS

Some of these poets
are seeing all the colors
& I'm seeing the blooming
of flowers in the colors
through their eyes,
the streaming of liquified poems,
psychedelically running down
through words and skin,
dripping from fingertips and lips,
down the shapes of bodies
and out and around
in sands
& soils
& lakes
& oceans
& little children
& concrete cities
& over and beyond
out into the depths of space.
Everything is so much,
so much much,
so so much
much.

27 JUNE 2021 — PAYNE COUNTY, OKLAHOMA

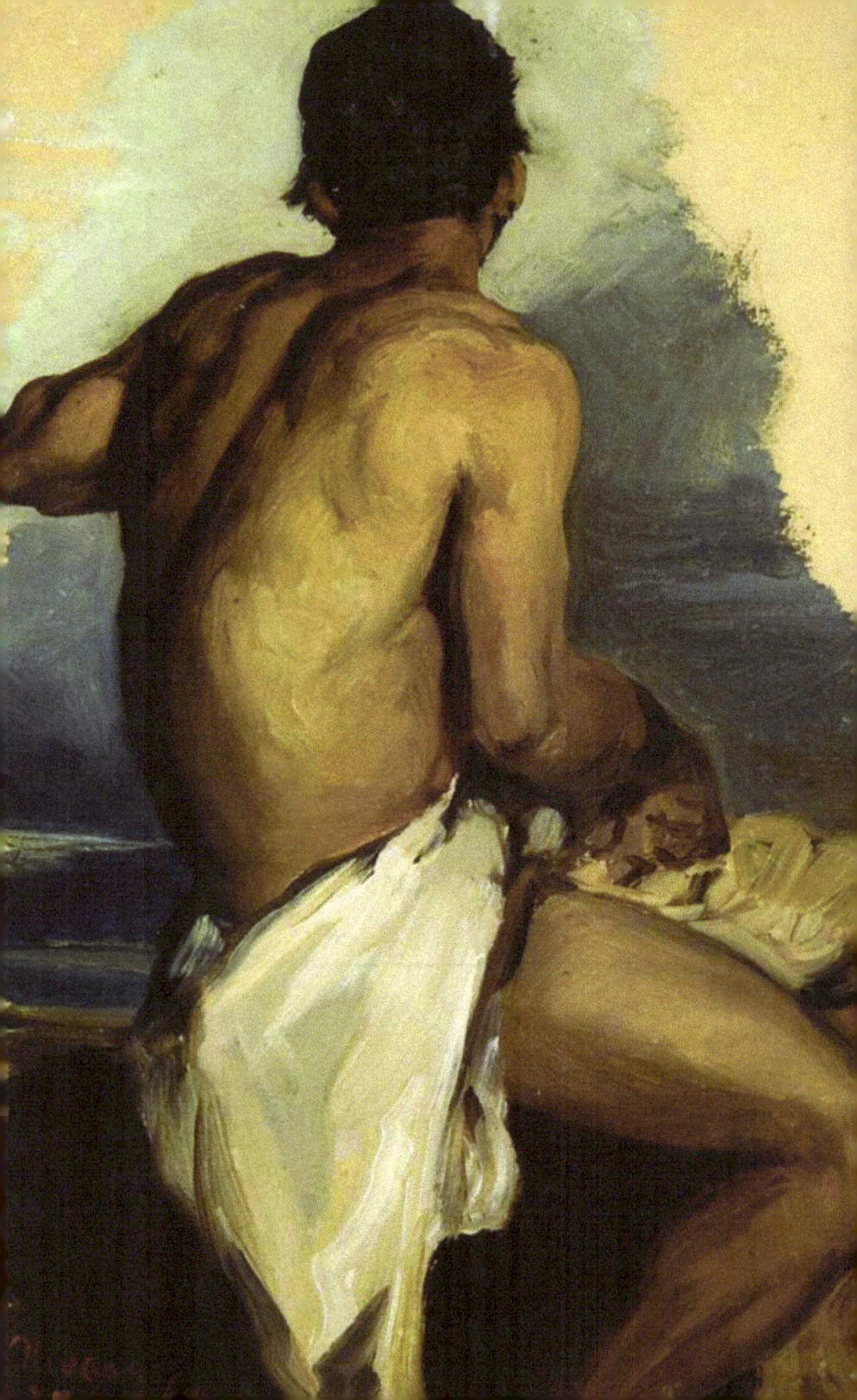

GOLDENROD

The cotton sheets fill with box fan air,
cooling our fires enough to contain the heat.
Sweat evaporates off our skin, so we try
even harder to create our own humidity.
I stay in bed all afternoon,
the fan blowing a rippling sheet
across the skin of my back,
tickling me like you before
you left me here with your ghost.
I drift in and out,
the fabric pattering gently.
I find so much comfort in the cold,
and in the dried sweat still clinging
to my body and my hair.
Outside a window,
goldenrod sways,
framed pleasingly in the window,
the fuchsia lace of far-off
crape myrtle just accenting
the yellow of the swaying wildflowers.
This is my reward for neglect,
a beautiful eruption of prairie.
Goldenrod is such a delicate friend,
blowing easily in the lightest wind,
often flattened by late August, still a-bloom.
It keeps me company on the long afternoons
of your absence.
I eventually shower, washing your minerals
from my hair and from my skin,

the water rinsing the remnants away.
I return to the bedroom,
to a book by James Schuyler.
The goldenrod is so proud this year,
standing tall, panicles bursting
with wild velvet just waiting
to be harvested, to be used
in a luxurious sofa
where we can wrap together, overwinter.
Every now and then, a shimmer-
ing ruby throated hummingbird,
Archilochus colubris,
hovers and laboriously drinks
nectar from the soft petals.
They are made of a different velvet,
crushed and almost metallic,
but still so soft.
They move on quickly;
this flower is not as generous as it is lovely,
its nectar reserved for painted ladies,
checkerspots,
fritillaries,
bumblebees as velvety-soft
as the flowers themselves.
They rest on the spears,
and take their time on these long afternoons.
I wonder if they are waiting as well.
Velvet is a distraction anyway.
I've turned on the fan again,
the wafting softness of cotton sheets
once again frolic along the expanses of my skin
that waits for your return.

26 AUGUST 2020 — PAYNE COUNTY, OKLAHOMA

DEAD OF NIGHT

It's all been waiting,
          waiting,
          waiting.

I knew where to find myself,
and I knew who I wanted.

But here I am, waiting.
I knew where to lose myself,
where to become a human person.

The view from my window
is obscured and beyond, pasture.
My skin has forgotten
some of my lovers.

It's difficult for men to find
a hermit sitting in a box in
the middle of rural America,
writing words for Canadians.

My muscles are exhausted
from the time spent building
the wrong temples—waiting,
          waiting,
          waiting.

for Emily Salt
inspired by the Orville Peck song

25 MARCH 2021 — PAYNE COUNTY, OKLAHOMA

A True Account of Talking to the Sun at Fire Island [24]

I can still feel your skin on my hands. [25]
I feel so lost I don't see the light; [26]
behind the wheel the hungry tiger's [27]
freckling under the sweet sun.. [28]

When you put on the mask the thunder starts [29]
and the world cracked and all things were reborn. [30]
We rose up, naked and rampant, [31]
& you may ask if hunger is the only passion, [32]
or is it also NOW you fear the tigers will eat you? [33]

You leave the same impression. [34]
Let it part your thighs, [35]
take root in my mouth; [36]
I must have noticed your lips touch mine. [37]
But life is short, —too short to be apart. [38]
A rainbow comes pouring into my window, I am electrified. [39]
Quickly climb closer and kiss me on the face, [40]
and make love under twinkling constellations. [41]
This queer sex book is not very dirty. [42]
Tonite I am reading books & remembering our old nights
together naked— [43]
your sandpaper beard against my face, [44]
my thumb flicking a nipple hard as ice. [45]
My body entwined with yours to end the possibility. [46]

a cento remnant for lovers

28 MARCH 2021 — PAYNE COUNTY, OKLAHOMA

I'D LIKE HIM TO WEAR BOOTS

(sometimes), thinking they are sexy.

If only for a moment, I should receive happiness. People seem happy when they are in love and I just go about my business pretending not to notice.

Shake me   Let's go back to sleep in each other's arms.
Winter is long and too many cold night will keep happiness sounding like a foreign language, unless we never leave this place. Can you even hear me? Even this will one day feel like a distant memory. How lucky other people are, I think, watching your closed eyes dart back and forth. How lucky we are, I guess.

I want to feel taken (for granted).

Sexy, side sore, pierced with arrows;

nothing ever seems to heal,
least of all my
       heart.

If beauty is on the inside, then rip me open & make love to my carcass. Everything is so random, so predetermined. Discard me, disregard me, ignore me until you need me.

I have secrets to whisper in your ear.

TULIP-KING

thrown petal from
p
     e
         t
             a
                 l

wrapped   around
              in
              on
              dark comforts of hats,

hats of hats
hat-hats of hats

s-p-l-a-y-e-d   p-u-r-p-l-e

two lips
pulled apart,

a song sung for the ghosts
& shadows that move through
the ridges of grey matter.

Breathing,
two lips,

erupting in fire
of wasps

Engulfed in morning shadows
& merriment of hat songs,
tulip shadows, ghost wasps,

f
i
r
e

Tulip-king
the fire of ten thousand wasps,
erupting through every known
volcano,
singing
two lips
with hats.

for Justin on his birthday
14 JULY 2021 — PAYNE COUNTY, OKLAHOMA

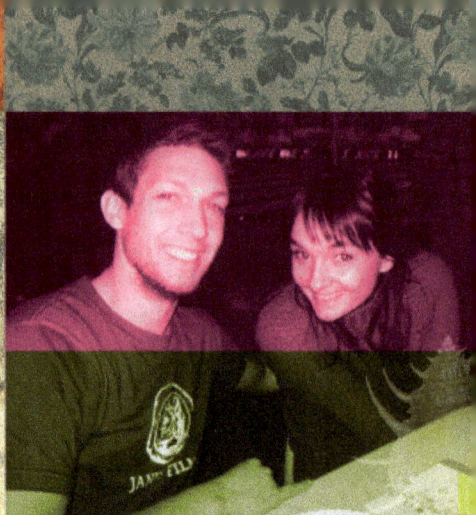

KEVIN HAWKINS

/ˈkɛvɪn ˈhɔ kɪnz/

noun

1. A self-portrait by Édouard Vuillard.

2. The grief left in a space where William Aalto should have been, mourned in the flowers of James Schuyler's pen.

3. The dawn chorus—a thousand unseen birds in the cottonwood trees

4. A statue on the seafloor of the Mediterranean, the coveted Greek treasure of elusive monk seals basking on Aegean coasts.

5. A kiss left on Kerith's lips.

23 OCTOBER 2020 — ANCHORAGE, ALASKA

ORIGINALLY APPEARED IN *MUSKOX VS. UNICORN* (2020)

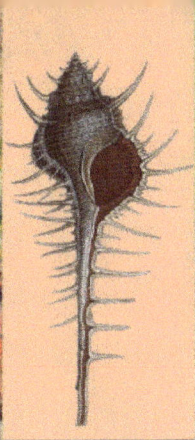

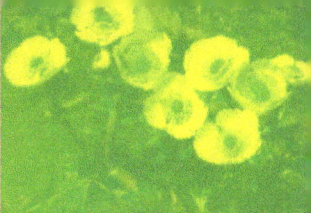

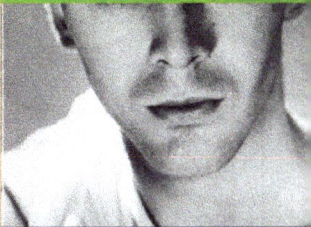

IS SAND & STARS

WITH KERITH HAWKINS

Surely you are bound and entwined,
You are mingled with the elements unborn;
I have loved a stream and a shadow. [47]
                    — *Ezra Pound*

<u>1</u>
love is a thing,
the best thing
love is the most thing
love is
          (especially kevin's)
more equal   more
more

we follow the stars
along our beaches,

following
how & what,
flowing in & out
of each other

2
we were not as,
we were   at first,
immediately

love is full of stars
          & of beach sand & of more

it was (   ) the first night,
          everyone asleep,
          holding her

          alone

i didn't think of love

the air's full of sand,
& we follow the stars,
our eyes shut wide open

3
i am so happy
that love is as is,
& isn't as was

i am so happy
this isn't what
my parents had

~~i am so happy~~
~~with everything~~
~~i've become~~

i am so happy
to be filled with
stardust and sand

<u>4</u>
last night
i held her   (alone)
we giggled at beach rocks
stuck between toes
& i thought only
of love,
of is

<u>5</u>
i stayed in her bed,
at last deep in our ocean
beyond stars & beaches

(as she slept) i felt her
soft dewy breath on my chest

her eyes were closed,
following the stars,
exactly like kevin's,
asleep,
more,
love,
is

10 JULY 2021 — HOMER, ALASKA
PAYNE COUNTY, OKLAHOMA

A WILD WOMAN

"This grand show is eternal. It is always sunrise somewhere; the dew is never dried all at once; a shower is forever falling; vapor is ever rising. Eternal sunrise, eternal dawn and gloaming, on sea and continents and islands, each in its turn, as the round earth rolls." [48]

— *John Muir*

Coreopsis is blooming along the spidering
　　　　network of open roads,
hidden in the wild pockets
　　　　under Congress Avenue Bridge,
restlessly waiting, as we all have, for the bursting
　　　　exuberance of bats
in the the full breadth of their congress
　　　　in Summer's dusk.
Some nights are filled with a great hunger,
　　　　a longing,

& she satiates like turnip greens,
　　　　like a hearty campfire-cooked meal.

Mountains call them, draw them
        from those humid homelands,
inviting two lovers to retrace
        the expansions that existed before,
connecting them to generations
        of bats, deer, bobcats, their own children.
He almost can't stand to look at her;
        she's become so beautiful.
Explorations suspend time,
        the two enveloped in perfect moments.
Light shines through the cathedral windows
        on her arms, onto
each thigh tattooed
        with their own cave paintings

gleaned from every explored cave,
        every canyon,
enthusiastically carved
        onto each other's hearts.
Nothing else exists,
        but two entwined souls gently wrapped together.
Zephyrs make the coreopsis sway,
        highway gardens in gentle ballet.
August is always full of surprises;
        it strengthens their bond to the
rivers, the rocks, the sun that shone
        so brilliantly on her skin.
Dawn is always erupting over the horizon;
        she's a nymph
in repose, a painting by Titian,
        the full synthesis of his purpose.

for Chris & Michele Genzardi

23 DECEMBER 2020 — PAYNE COUNTY, OKLAHOMA

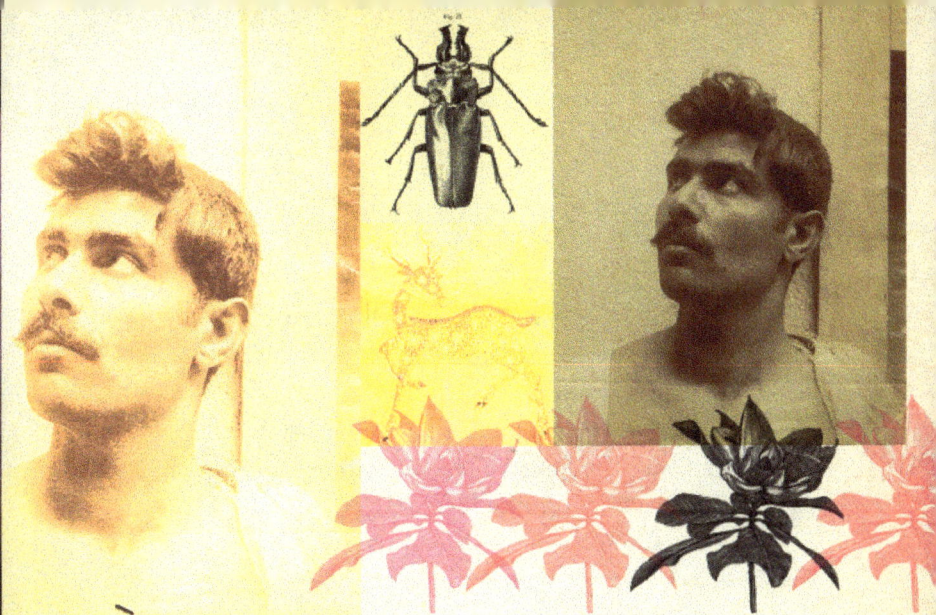

LAWRENCE FERLINGHETTI IS DEAD

*"I shall take the liberty to champion whom and what I please,
and your royal highness will be obliged to stand it, and with no
back talk"* [49]

—Caroline Churchill, The Queen Bee

We've got homegrown voids,
sad spaces from coast to coast
where giants once stomped
forming breast-stroke-ready impressions
in the tranquility of mid-century upheaval,
but now erosion and time
will transform those pools into mere suggestions
of feet—faint outlines of their full enormity.
The natural eschewing of greatness
may prove fatal for the legacy
of the Third Millennium.

Each toppled titan revealing the truth
and our lack of rising mountains.
Lawrence Ferlinghetti is dead now,
schlepping with him the meaning of literature,
the poetic heritage of an entire century.
The form itself sighed in verse,
crushed now by the weight of vapid puerility,
by downstrokes, by keystrokes, by counterstrokes,
by a general lack of experience,
and by a gleeful acceptance of ignorance.
Aesthetics run amok. Run so far amok
that they're cloyingly sticking in our throats,
clogging up the spaces around our uvulas,
choking out the importance of verisimilitude.
I'm writing this all for Emily Sugar,
for Millie Äpfelsäure,
for Melissa Chalky-Earth,
for Yemelyan Monosodium Glutamate,
YMSG for short, for sure, forever,
or just Emily.
Ferlinghetti is dead, that's undeniable,
but so too are Jack Kerouac,
Langston Hughes, Sylvia Plath,
Maya Angelou,
and Leonard Cohen.
But we're all eminently satisfied with you,
Emily Salt,
skulking down the spines of their oeuvres,
dipping your supple digits in the waters
where heroes and acolytes learned
to form the syllables of their work,
and where they celebrated one another.
You're sauntering along streams

where they fell in love with the spaces between,
and where they first penned their expressions
of devotion.
You're trying on the expressions of their devotions,
peering through the cavities of their skulls
to expand yourself and pull yourself in new directions.
What can I offer to show my own devotion?
How do I find a vocabulary for the praise,
for well-earned adulation and glorification?
Given the penchant for salinity,
I thought of starting with something to sate,
some pleasing morsels for your actual appetite:
potato latkes perhaps, at least to start,
or broccolini, puréed avocado,
maybe a bottle of eggy Avocaat.
Cacao and rambutan martinis are perhaps too fancy;
I should stick with rich cocoa and beer,
and maybe a soothing joint.
Suddenly, everyone is reading my words again.
I wish I had written this all in dactylic hexameter,
treated the salt with the reverence
reserved for a pontifex or a madame.
Maybe the verses would have sounded better
ripped from lines of *The Iliupersis*
or from symbols found carved in stone at Thebes.
I'm searching the spaces
between Whitby and the Osage Nation.
There must be a gift to present,
a present to offer that speaks clearly of my feelings.
Lawrence Ferlinghetti is dead.
Maybe you'd have preferred a simple quotation,
some lines of the newly deceased centenarian.
Poets don't go out in puffs of exasperated irrelevance,

drawing raised eyebrows when folks who first
read his words in a stuffy University
forty-some-odd years ago,
realize now they'd been breathing the same air
for all these years.
They'd never really thought about it,
and now the atmosphere feels saturated with his cells.
But I'm still focused on succession just now.
Sing for us Emily!
Dance along the lakeshore.
Hold a pose and I'll have Claude Ponsot
unbury himself in Hyde Park; what the worms left
behind will paint your form like he had painted Selden,
in phthalo blue, yellow ochre, keppel,
lavender, catawba, ecru,
carmine lake, and viridian.
He'll include bright cerulean skies filled
with flocks of vermillion pyrocephalus,
lush gardens dotted with magenta heliotropes
and heliotrope rhododendrons.
He'll use every hue, every pleasing shade,
ombré fields of complimentary colors.
And if I'm engaged in necromancy anyway,
maybe you'd just prefer Paul Kane.
I don't really know how patriotic you feel,
or maybe you'd be more comfortable
as one of Agnes Martin's subtle abstractions.
Just let me know.
In the meantime, I'll fashion for you an effigy
of Bragi from the fossilized phalanges
of the pterosaur Quetzalcoatlus,
adorned with plumes from a long extinct hoatzin
found in the Monkey Beds of Villavieja, Colombia.

I'll pick flowers for you,
everything from the commonplace
Taraxacum officinale to the rarest
Paphiopedilum fairrieanum,
branches of bougainvillea and even more
exotic *Nyctaginaceae*,
Mennegoxylong & *Reichenbachia hirsuta*,
phantasmic and ethereal blooms
of long lost genera
or blooms so rare as to only live in myth,
blossoms of the lotus tree that separates the heavens
from everything beyond.
I'll include eight April-bright branches in a bouquet.
A shrine feels appropriate.
We need to address the botanical lexicography
that keeps me isolated from you,
keeps me searching for flowers.
Emily, oh Emily!

You must be confused or drunk.
I have chosen for you only the gentlest words
in an effort to praise you.
None of this was my fault.
I was entranced by talent,
intoxicated by my perceptions.
I'm starting to check my watch,
but faint sounds are rising through
absurdly cartoonish Pacific streets,
through drumbeats and reefer-smoke.
Fuck! Emily, you just think you own everything,
don't you? I can't say you're wrong,
not while throwing myself at your feet.
Burn it all.
Tear down everything.
There was hardly any glory in the rowdy flamboyance,
and you shine as bright any day of the week.
Show these kids how trite their efforts have been.
Puce. I forgot to mention the puce
of a raggedy davenport in an old coffee shop.
Maybe this wasn't terribly important to mention,
and maybe most of this never happened.
The air is thick with what I can only assume
is your intention to pick up the goddamn mic
and blow us all into the next century.
And we certainly need someone to do it.
Lawrence Ferlinghetti,
as you may have heard,
is dead.

for Emily Salt
7 MARCH 2021 — PAYNE COUNTY, OKLAHOMA

MARCONA ALMONDS

I'm trying to rewind time, pull back,
force myself

      to fall

in love with you,
or at least your words,
even though I know I'm making mistakes
and hurting myself,
or you.

He's still back there in the past,
studying your skin,
blushing Marcona almonds,
writing poetry about your smile,
dreaming about the inside of your brain.

I wonder if you are meant to be here,
if we prepared for you sufficiently.

He's still back there in the past,

      overthinking

      everything.

It's all platonic, these words,
but sometimes they feel much stronger
like I've lost all control of myself.
I don't even understand platonic anymore.
Everything is so much more,
heightened by an urgency to...

It's going by too fast.

I'm trying to rewind time,
find you at the start,
we've missed so much time already,
I'm sure there were things I wanted to say,
secrets I'd always kept to myself.

It's windy on these plains;
bindweed vines creep out,
spilling over everything in all directions,
except where you are.
I wonder what that means.
Perhaps you've had nymph troubles,
and haven't we all?

Do the gods know you are here? Or
did they misplace you when they fell

in love
with the words you wrote
and with your eyes?

Entranced.

for Jairo Dealba

1 JUNE 2021 — PAYNE COUNTY, OKLAHOMA

THE CIRCLE

BY JAIRO DEALBA

I lie sick in waiting
For the kiss
That will end
With existence

Yet I am trembling in a cause
That makes me not
Understand
The meaning of my life

But
In love
There is a chance
To protrude
And widen the gap
Because my mouth
Is a circle

And I still lie sick
With the beads
Of my sweat
Clearing my skin
In a bed of sorrows
And pasts defied

5 JULY 2021 — LINDON, UTAH

Invisible Spiders

I lie sick in waiting
for a touch
that is always
just beyond reach

Yet my skin is a thousand
invisible spiders
eagerly preparing
for Winter

But
in skittering
they've neglected
their webs
for collecting
my escaped rational
thoughts

And I will lie sick
exposed to the cold
of my own torment
The last gossamer bits
disappearing
with my memories

after Jairo Dealba, "The Circle"

6 JULY 2021 — PAYNE COUNTY, OKLAHOMA

A KALEIDOSCOPE

You are the loosened bit
of down, shed on
a young bird's first migration,
a patch of soft grass
where the lost feather
will dance in stray breezes
before getting down to the serious
business of decomposition,
dissipating into nutrients,
food for sleeping seeds
waiting for Spring
when they will germinate,
reach their spindly arms to the sun
as if they'll be able to pull it down
& devour it themselves.
You are the worn whelk shell,
washed slowly to shore,
eaten away by the grinding sand,
the spark of a child's imagination,
the souvenir of romantic lovers,
the reminder of those we've lost.
You are my ego's muse & my muse's ego,
a perpetual force of pen and paper,
a skilled forger of beating hearts,
of quaking hearts,

of lost & found hearts,
lost & found wanderers,
troubadours, beachcombers,
hopeless romantics,
new generations ready to slice
themselves open with their sharpest
pens & finely crafted keyboards.
They're readying themselves
to catch the spilling of truths
you've encouraged across all generations
and across the drifting clouds.
You are a giant; you are the giant,
a towering force of inspiration
& a humble force of compassion.
You are the wind that drives the clouds,
and the waves that drive our dreams.
You are more than these things,
more than your realization allows.
You are more than blue,
more than the words written
in endless detailed journals in your youth.
You are purple and yellow,
the vastness of green,
the red blood pumping through
a community of iron-clad artists,
the clarity of salty tears.
You are more than every rainbow
of every spoken truth,
of every unspoken secret.
You are a kaleidoscope, not only of colors,
but of our journeys and our revelations.

for Robert A. Cozzi

23 JUNE 2021 — PAYNE COUNTY, OKLAHOMA

Skin

Whose skin is this?
These tattoos have spread out,
leaking into spaces around them
& I'm wondering if the snapshots
still tell my story,
still tell the story I wanted to be my story.
Have I become the person I meant to become
when I asked for these decorations?
Whose memories are these,
captured in disinterested ink?
Memories fade, spread out
into the moments around them,
& it's all become so muddy and singular.
My youth moves slowly,
a glacier creeping through my dermal layers.
Whose skin is this?
My hands are wrapped in the same skin
that my grandma's hands had been,
wrinkled and soft and beautiful.
My face is settling into the form
that my dad's face has settled into,
wrinkled and soft and well…
if not beautiful, then kindly perhaps.
My arms are spotted with the same freckles
that my mom's arms had been,
wrinkled and sun-kissed and beautiful.
Whose skin is this?
Whose memories?
Am I still in here?

24 JUNE 2021 — PAYNE COUNTY, OKLAHOMA

LIGHTNING BUGS

It hasn't been enough.
I grasp at people,
lightning bugs I want to jar,
to admire and keep close.

They've been too quick,
darting and evading me,
lighting up and confusing me.
Everyone feels so far away.

15 MAY 2008 — ANCHORAGE, ALASKA

122

NOSTALGIC STRAGGLE

I don't remember tethering myself to youth like this,
but I keep wandering too far away,
the cords tugging me back off my feet.
Everything seems different with the decades,
somehow not right and somehow better.
If I find a knife, will I even try to cut myself free?
This restraint is almost as comforting as those youthful lies.

The boys are as beautiful as they ever were,
full-bearded and bald,
twice-married,
fathers.
Grandfathers.
If I had unwound myself at the right moments,
maybe they'd look out their windows
and wonder about me.

25 MARCH 2021 — PAYNE COUNTY, OKLAHOMA

A Tiger; A Corsair; A Lamb [50]

Flowers are blossoming as a woodpecker plays a drum solo, [51]
sweet memories of another age. [52]
I could imagine myself picking daisies [53]
as I slowly sink to the bottom. [54]

I've been self-destructing, slowly, since the womb. [55]

You can't tame wildflowers, [56]
but flowers sing better than us [57]
after the cries of the birds has stopped. [58]

These are my companions for life, & they love me.
But you pay and you pay and you pay; [59]
What else can I do to soften these edges? [60]
The Tiger-Woman's voice was sweet; [61]
a tamed beast has lost its power. [62]

The sky sinks down in summertime, to rest, [63]
and climbs half way down. But there's also a tiger below. [64]
Looks like the sky. The sky looks tiger striped; [65]
the disordered heavens, ragged, ripped by winds. [66]

We can come to terms with the heavens. [67]
Eternity must be hiding back there, it's done so before. [68]

a cento remnant for Travis Latham & J.D. Winterhalter

6 MAY 2021 — PAYNE COUNTY, OKLAHOMA

A SLICE OF PUMPKIN PIE

it was never   enough & years from now
                memories will catch me
                silly & blurry

love teetered   so long, never as stable
                so beautifully, never as lovely
                perfectly imperfect

we feel it   in the pits of our stomachs
    and so suddenly nothing seems to fit
    everything pushes apart
    our continents shift
    in great earthquakes

    we had started to eat
    before the pie had set
    & those earthquakes
    opened rifts where
    stones were lodged
& our family started falling
one by one into the abyss

hardly even a crumb
remains of succulence
of rich sweetness
of love

25 AUGUST 2009 — ANCHORAGE, ALASKA

DISCOVERING YOUR BOTANY

You are my warm fertile soil,
      enriched & fed by countless pink-
      brown worms, the fingers of your strong hands
You are my sun-thirsty leaves,
      unfurling, soaking in daylight,
      lovingly photosynthesizing
You are my protective bark,
      sheltering my soft parts from the
      harshness, hugging my body tightly.
You are a thousand blossoms,
      the bursting exuberance of
      Winter's end on my green-flushed branches.
You are the buzzing of bees,
      a song sung at the entrance to
      my nectaries, my petals open.
You are the reason I bloom,
      the reason I extend my roots
      and why I break dormancy each Spring.

17 SEPTEMBER 2020 — PAYNE COUNTY, OKLAHOMA
ORIGINALLY APPEARED IN *SCISSORTAIL QUARTERLY* #2 (MARCH 2021)

Fairy Boy

Adrift as
        dandelion parasols

float
        float
                float

menfolk are too far
menfolk are too
men-folk
too men, aggress
        ive too too too buff
             (dull dull dull)

So, drift

the fields glitter sunlit dew

your skin glitters
        blushed dots
        fallen stars
        firefly kisses
        my fingerprints

ALL green blushes
flushes
rushes
green
aglow in green

painted little leaf-buds
popping up little leaf-buds
       popping out little leaf-buds
              pop-pop
              & then trees

god, I love glitter-
      y faces
      flushing & blushing
      popping buds, popping
      sparkled smiles
      speckled, sweet hums
      buds

menfolk are too much men
oiled & entangled
      slip-slip-slip
      oh, muscles
      slippery games
menfolk, too much, overly
      writhing so naked
      so irked, overly
      so pressed, overly
      so squinty-eyed, overly
      so manly, too much overly

Ah, float
      iridescent wings

drift
      drift
            drift

god, I love blue
dragonflies
your hair

& pink & black
& street art
magic
& everything stretching
beyond
cerise lips

menfolk are much too much
too, too manly
short-shorts ballet
lithe choreography
"10 men with sphere"
such lovely dancing
& flamboyant

Magical creature
bloom pink
& petals
dance in beyonds
beyond beyonds
past beyond beyonds
soft little buds

paint magic on the sun
float
float
float

1 JULY 2021 — PAYNE COUNTY, OKLAHOMA

NOCTURNE

"Midnight shakes the memory
As a madman shakes a dead geranium." [69]
— *T. S. Eliot*

Lately, I've stayed up with the moon,
sitting uneasily in the cool Spring breeze,
chuck-will's-widow calling through the night.
On & on & on through the darkness the bird cries.

My demons join me, slipped through shadows,
hanging in branches of nearby trees to hide,
as though I won't notice them there.
They forget how heavily their breaths escape,
and about the heat of their fiery bellies.

I'm glad the demons are here with me,
otherwise I'd just have the moon for company,
and the sad, wailing bird.
They aren't very good company;
the moon blankly staring
down at me, tracing my every movement
like an old woman whose cataracts
have become her way of life.
And that nightjar has been carrying on for so long

It's lonely in the night, with this moon aloft & aloof.
Nobody can see how eagerly I let the demons whisper,
how I bend toward them with a yearning for heat.
My longings are sculpted and beautiful;
if they could, they'd fill my house with life,
my bed with warmth,
my skin.

I'm no good at being in the night.
My body comes to life as the sun erupts,
spilling pink light through the trees.
It's hard to stay concealed in those rays,
my true form lighting up,
betraying me.

30 MAY 2021 — PAYNE COUNTY, OKLAHOMA

HOP OFF, LITTLE LAPIN

hop hop skip skip hop hop skip!
little flowered
bunny-eared...   sugarsugar
                    hi!

bounce bounce jump jump jump!
cute-in-white
halo-clad...   curtsy for the audience.

clap clap yell yell clap clap clap!
carbonated
caffeinated   coffeecoffee
                    more!

wave wave bye bye bye!
don't forget me...
I won't forget you jenniejennie

            babe!

for Jennie Lloyd
6 APRIL 1999 — TULSA, OKLAHOMA

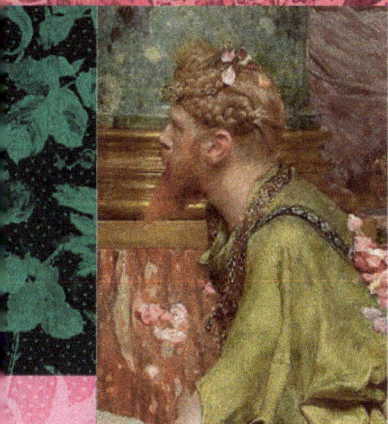

A New Cloak for the Occasion

37.
I had made myself a home in a forest,

returned to Oklahoma to find myself, to find Mom, to understand a man who had begun to fade away from us, forgetting our names, losing the words, becoming increasingly

translucent.

I stood vigil among the trees   after he was gone and then witnessed the fading of my own parents and the pulling away of the niblings who turned aloof and estranged, as children do. Their lives lay in front of them.

Elagabalus' specter whispered to me through the trees,

lured me into the forest with a promise of fabled orgies, now attended as they always should have been, by the ghosts of only the best deities — Agni, Mwari, Apollo. I looked for them among the prickly pears and pecan trees, cutting myself badly on the thorns of a young honey locust.

Youth is like that sometimes,

and I imagined the thorns of my own,
the chiffon
pierced
and
torn,

the peach stained with dirt and blood.

That cut would nearly kill me, and I spent much of my time recovering with the voices rising from the trees of the gathering I could never find.

The birds told me secrets,
but I did not understand their languages.

I would talk to Xōchipilli through the blooms of a garden that I could not tame, that I longed to tame, and which I would soon look past when my heart was at last ripped from my chest and fed to the great nothingness at the final exhalation of my mother's breath.

The ripped and stained chiffon was replaced by a cloak

of dried leaves

and I took comfort in the smell of rot
and in the sow bugs hiding under every leaf.

I can still see the ripped sky
with my eyes closed,

the green bands of light,
the snow,
the stars,
the star.

I imagine it all as I left it, grown over and free of that man I had
become, and of those friends who thought I was too naïve to
notice.

The strength has returned,
the mangled legs now scarred,
ruined.

I want to grow antlers, hooves, wings, a beautiful face for others
to admire, distractions from everything that has gone wrong,
join the beauty I imagine, just there in the trees,

the communion of gods,

of beautiful men,
of flowers.

Someday I will find those rifts,
climb the jagged peaks of those mountains
and slip through,
my body turning to stars and snow,
spilling out on either side,
a trail of peach chiffon
slipping across the sky.

7 APRIL 2020 — PAYNE COUNTY, OKLAHOMA
A VERSION ORIGINALLY APPEARED IN *SOCIAL DISTANCES* (2020)

ਅੰਬ-ਦਿਲ ਦਾ ਰਾਜਾ

ਸੰਗੀਤ ਧਰਤੀ ਦੀ ਗਹਿਰਾਈ ਤੋ ਉੱਠਦਾ ਹੈ,
ਹਰ ਰੁੱਖ ਦੀਆਂ ਜੜ੍ਹਾ ਦੁਆਰਾ ਖਿੱਚਿਆ ਜਾਂਦਾ ਹੈ,
ਗੁਲਾਬ ਦੀ ਛੰਡੀ ਦੀ ਸ਼ਾਖਾ ਦੁਆਰਾ,
ਪੁਰਾਣੇ ਪੀਪਲ ਦੇ ਹਰੇ ਦਲਿਆ ਦੁਆਰਾ
ਜਨਵਰੀ ਦੀ ਕੜਕਦੀ ਥਪਾਂ ਵਿੱਚ ਧਾਕ ਦੁਆਰਾ
ਇਹ ਪੱਕ ਅੰਬਾ ਦੇ ਟਪਕਦ ਰਸ ਵਿੱਚ ਗੂੰਜਦਾ ਹੈ,
ਸਾਡੇ ਸਰੀਰ ਦੇ ਅੰਦਰ ਚੱਲ ਰਹੀ ਮਠਿਆਸ ਹੈ,
ਸਾਡੇ ਕੰਪਤੀਆ ਵਿੱਚ ਰਸ ਜਾਂਦਾ ਹੈ।
ਇਹ ਸਾਡੇ ਸਪਨਿਆ ਵਿੱਚ ਗੂੰਜਦਾ ਹੈ ਅਤੇ ਸਾਡੇ ਨੂੰ
ਮਿਲਿਉਦਾ ਹੈ।
ਸਾਡੀਆਂ ਖਾਸ ਰੱਖੀਆ ਯਾਦਾ ਨੂੰ ਤਾਜਾ ਕਰਦਾ ਹੈ
ਧਿਆਨ ਰੱਖੋ! ਸੋਮੇ ਦੀ ਮੌਜੂਦਗੀ ਵਿੱਚ ਸੰਗਮਰਮਰ ਦੇ ਰਸ
ਜਿਵੇਂ ਉਹ ਹਰ ਚੀਜ ਵੱਚੋ ਲੰਘਦਾ ਹੈ,
ਜਿਵੇਂ ਉਹ ਗੂੰਜਦਾ ਹੈ।
ਉਸਦੇ ਖੂਬਸੂਰਤ ਫਲਾ ਦੀ ਅਵਾਜ,
ਅਤੇ ਸਾਡੇ ਪੂਰਵਜਾ ਦੀਆ ਭਾਸ਼ਾਵਾ ਦੁਆਰਾ
ਕੀ ਹੁਣ ਪੁਰਾਰਥਨਾ ਕਰਨ ਦਾ ਸਮਾਂ ਹੈ?
ਮੈ ਆਪਣਾ ਹੱਥ ਜਮੀਨ ਤੇ ਵੈਲਾ ਰਹੀ ਹਾ
ਦਲਿ ਦੀ ਧੜਕਨ, ਇਸਦੇ ਕੰਬਣ ਵਾਲੇ ਸਵਰੂਪ ਨੂੰ ਮਹਿ
ਲਈ
ਉਸ ਕੋਰਸ ਨੂੰ ਜਿਸਨੇ ਗਾਉਣਾ ਸੁਰ ਕੀਤਾ
ਰਸੀਲੇ ਫਲਾ ਦੇ ਪੱਕਣ ਤੇ ਪਹਿਲਾ,
ਅਮਰਤਾ ਤੋ ਵੱਖ ਹੋਣ ਤੋ ਪਹਿਲਾ
ਮੈ ਸੰਕੇਤਾ ਲਈ ਤਾਰਾ ਨੂੰ ਆਸਮਾਨ ਦੇਖ ਰਹੀ ਹਾ,
ਤੋਤਿਆਂ ਦੇ ਝੁੰਡ ਇਕੱਠੇ ਕਰਨ ਲਈ
ਆਪਣੇ ਕਟਕਦੇ ਭਰਾ ਦੀ ਢਾਲ ਵਿੱਚ,
ਇਕੱਲੇ ਐਲਬੈਟਰੋਸ ਲਈ, ਇੱਕ ਅੰਤ ਤੋ ਨਿਕਲਿਆ
ਸਾਡੀ ਨੀਂਦ ਵਿੱਚ ਗਾਏ ਗਏ ਗੀਤਾ ਦੁਆਰਾ ਪਰਫੁੱਲ
ਸੰਗੀਤ ਧਰਤੀ ਦੀ ਗਹਿਰਾਈ ਤੋ ਉੱਠ

MANGO-HEARTED KING

The music rises from Earth's depths,
drawn through the roots of every tree,
through the branching of the rosewoods,
through the green hearts of ancient peepals,
through the erupting flames of a January dhak.
It hums in the dripping juice of ripe mangoes,
the sweetness running down our bodies,
soaking into our clothes.
It hums in our dreams, shifting our hands,
vibrating our carefully placed memories.
Be careful! Don't forget to wear marble
in the presence of time
as he flows through everything,
as he reverberates through
the vocal cords of his beautiful fruits,
and through the languages of our ancestors.
Is it time to pray yet?
I'm stretching out my hand across the ground
to feel the heartbeat, the vibrating patterns
of the chorus that started singing
before the ripening of succulent fruits,
before the disconnection from immortality.
I'm watching the skies along the coasts for signs,
for the gathering flocks of parrots
looking for their wandering brother,
for a lone albatross, hatched from an egg
incubated by the songs sung in our sleep.
The music rises from Earth's depths,
drawn through the pens of poets
and through the vocal cords of kings.

for Kai

9 AUGUST 2021 — PAYNE COUNTY, OKLAHOMA

SPECIAL

The days starts with fruit,
with pineapple & melon. Everyone
knows that. Why does nothing
smell sweet this morning?
I'm too tired to dig out
a melon baller, too tired
to buy a fresh fruit.

There are no lakes anymore,
I'm pretty sure, no mountains
where we can sleep, & I'm so tired.
Everything is hiding in clouds,
and still it will not rain. When
did everything become so empty?

We've all lost our appetites
for the nostalgia that once dripped
down our young faces,
but I'd save a bite for anyone
if they'd bother to keep
thoughts of me close.

Half a kiwi is still too much,
I know, so nobody bothers to stop by
& I've lost all my Hawaiian decor.
This won't be much of a luau.
I'd fire up the grill, if I had one,
just in case anyone was hungry,
but I'm good. I'm never that hungry
anymore, never that interested
in waiting for people too full
for half a kiwi.

I'll probably nod off
to a movie I love after being
too patient for my own good.
I am so tired, but I got my own
cake, and I don't know
if they know that it is
big enough to share,
big enough to share,
big enough to share.
Do they know it is
big enough to share?

I'm checking my phone,
and don't worry, it's not you.
I'm just waiting for a call
that never seems to come.
Not anymore.
Why is it so quiet?

5 AUGUST 2021 — PAYNE COUNTY, OKLAHOMA

MINOTAUR

1
I'm still transfixed
by the invisible rainbows
where my reflection

drifted across the
grey junctions of spaces
too small to contradict

the meanings of words
we sometimes only
pretended to understand

I was deposited lightly
in the days of George Nigh
when a community

filled themselves with
the naïveté of joy and freedom
just before darkness settled

I watch the memories
of innocence, watch you
making waffle cones

or lies to convince others
to see you, to stop feeling
like you might slip into

the rainbow's invisible veils
drift across the grey spaces
where neighbors hide hate

like we can't see it
on their faces, lips pursed
as they strain to tolerate us

2

Mistakes have been made in these homes,
and there are wounds so deep that they can
never be properly healed, the bones exposed
in the gashes. I had seen you once, towering
so high above me, in the meaning of everything
I thought I might be, the freedom of existence
I imagined for myself before I knew
what myself meant. I fixed you in the sky,
the brightest star in a constellation
I knew I should never speak about,
and one I should always have spoken about.

3

We were a part of the night,
never full rainbows, but silvery
moths flitting toward the moon.

You could always see me,
always reached for my shoulder when
I'd slumped forward in darkness,

always finding me in the night
to remind me that the night is more
than darkness, more than moonlight.

We were formed and deposited,
the same bits of clay at the edge,
in grey spaces between everything

trying on rejection before it was
used to destroy us, and it was.
We were the light, and we still shine.

4

Incalculable mistrust, forgotten
or remembered inconsistencies,
six decades of piled up diversions,
        fantasies of unseen tethers,
        all fray, damp with venom.

It's no wonder you've filled everything
with your own applause, cajoled a world
into loving you like you feared you were
not worthy of being loved,
like you feared you could only hide
before they found and flogged
you to death with your flaws.

Every rainbow requires light,
and I am trying to remember
how we had first seen each other,
        melting until we saw ourselves,
        keeping quiet our deep secrets.

5

The clay is freckled & ruddy,
roots struggle to secure themselves.

You've always known how to prepare soil,
folding in the elements to foster growth.

Hands that hold earth are the purest hands,
even if they're nested securely in brambles.

I wonder if you've ever broken free,
if the thorns slice through skin like your words.

The clay is rusty & densely packed,
our buried birds struggle to break free.

for Stan

14 AUGUST 2021 — PAYNE COUNTY, OKLAHOMA

A THEORY OF TIGERS

The flames burn out of control,
an inferno of theoretical tigers,
plasma of imagination, warm
as Siberia in January & cool
as an August here where the plains
meet forests on Hell's rooftop,
where any large cat can slink in
& out of shadows, in
& out of existence.

The flames burn out of control,
an inferno of theoretical tigers,
suggestions & innuendo,
a mixture of fictions, of histories,
of detailed records kept
in the early morning hush
at the end of passions.
It's stopped mattering
if my words are real.

The flames burn out of control,
an inferno of theoretical tigers,
a sun trapped in a nest of clouds,
glowing pure orange light.
These words are the memories
of lives I might have lived.
They are a dreamer's manifesto.
Realities are unimportant;
poetry is my reality.

27 JUNE 2021 — PAYNE COUNTY, OKLAHOMA

AFTER WORD

THE PRESSURES OF TIME

Thunder is not thunder because it chose to fall upon the ground with ferocity. It chose to fall upon the ground because it was destined to do so. Thus in fervent sprite the world of poetry has been blissfully blessed with the chance for us to look at the world in a different kind of way: a more open way; a way that is filled without concern and sober uniqueness. Time has held its course since the beginning of its birth. The core of its blood resides in the silence of it all. Nothing in the end remains in silence, not because it doesn't want to. But because the world cannot move in it despite its own desire to move in disguise. When we speak about thunder, silence, and the universe, one can be so bored. But when we talk about poetry we are filled with the anticipation of the times. We are cursed with glorious anxiousness and rattled bodies. We consider it all, even the thought that such a notion of poetry can and will bring us the joy that we deserve. Take for example the greatest poets. They have wielded upon their hands the magic of weaving with words and silence for them has always been a companion. We think about the process of writing as creating a glorious thunder that falls upon the earth with mighty power and prowess. It is precisely sure that God himself, if you believe in such things, would perform the written art with a quill of light. He has done so many times under the pretext of saving his people. Poetry has truly emboldened the myth and mystery of its very own nature. Cruelty, on the other hand, has demanded that poets curse their tongues and their lives for whatever reason or another. The stigmas of the poet's life have plagued it since the day someone or something began to write the adventures of another. In creative measures we behold ourselves. We do so blindly. We consider the respect of time with the utmost sacredness. Thriving through the perpendicular horizon of its fields, vast as they might be, the world is created to set aside all pride. There are fevers rising upon the people of this planet, whether they'd be of any gender or color it does not matter. What matters is that we say what we feel with freedom. The pressures of time have shown us everything. True. It is reality that is considered, off the course, when all men go to face the muse but do not come back; some have most astoundedly come back to tell us about themselves, to tell us in a wave of nostalgia, sorrow, and so forth what it means to write with thunder. It is not under-writ, but over the page of sorrows. With a pen they have moved us to tears. And despite their modus operandi we conclude that his heart belongs to the earth and to the sky with a rainbow full of mercy and obsequious beauty. The universe thanks them. Because they have done what men from Robert Duncan to Allen Ginsberg to Harvey Milk have done: they have acted with the courage of their hearts, moving us to remember that we must understand that equality means not choice but compassion and understanding.

— JAIRO DEALBA

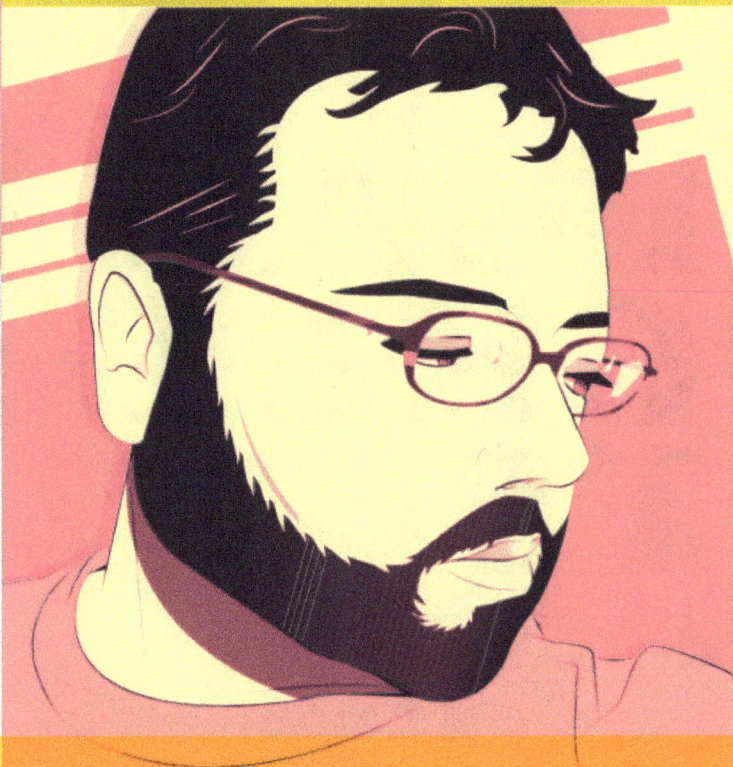

ABOUT THE AUTHOR

Brian Fuchs is the author of the poetry collections *Okie Dokie*, *Scissor-tailed Flycatcher*, & *Muskox vs. Unicorn*. He is the editor of *Scissortail Quarterly*, through which he has connected to many emerging new voices in poetry. Brian's work has appeared in the award-winning anthology *Perspective To Pen*, among others.

Brian is the editor-in-chief at Scissortail Press, and the CEO of over-complicating projects in his own life. He currently lives and works in rural Oklahoma, just outside of his hometown of Stillwater.

IMAGE CREDITS

All images used with permission.

Design & Layout by Brian Fuchs.

Primary image sources: 1. Photos from the personal collection of the author; 2. Wikimedia Commons (commons.wikimedia.org); 3. The Graphics Fairy (thegraphicsfairy.com).

Individual image credits:

front cover & p.36: Wilhelm von Gloeden, n.0174 (c.1895-1900); p.ii: Alexey Tyranov, "Мужской портрет" ("Portrait of a Man")(19th century); p.v: William Bruce Ellis Ranken, "The Garden Door" (1926); unknown artist, Korean tiger & magpie painting (altered), unknown artist, "Hemisodorcus nepalensis" (1912, The Fauna of British India); p.vii: Wilhelm von Gloeden, n.1590 "Adolescente laureato" (c.1895-1900); p.viii: Frances Benjamin Johnston, "Man posed on rocks, nude, playing pipe (Pan)" (c.1885-1900); p.xii: Wilhelm von Gloeden, "Mandorli in fiore" (before 1893); p.xiii: John R. Neill, endpaper illustration from The Sea Fairies by L. Frank Baum (1911); p.xv: John Singer Sargent, "Study for 'History'" (1916-1921); p. xvi: Franz Marc, "Deer at Dusk" (1909); p.2: Vincent Van Gogh, "Pear Tree in Blossom" (1888); p.3: Carel Fabritius, "The Goldfinch" (1654); Franz von Lenbach, "Porträt des Kronprinzen Rupprecht von Bayern" (c.1874); Paul Signac, "The Pine Tree at St. Tropez" (1909); unknown artist, "Rhododendron arborescens" (1913, An Illustrated Flora of the Northern United States, Canada and British Possessions by N.L. Britton & A. Brown); pp.4-5: photo of author (from personal collection); p. 6 Aurora132001, "Red Heron" (CC, Wikimedia); p.8: Edervan Farias de Jesus, "Eddy_Suryts" (CC, Wikimedia); p.10: Konrad Mägi "Lilleline väli majakesega" (c.1907); p.11: Alexandre Cabanel, "Fallen Angel" (1847); p.11 & various pages throughout: unknown artist, "The Tiger Lily" textile (1886); p.12: Homoparet, "Två män som kysser varandra hemma" (2010); p.14: photo of unknown sailor; shell illustration (graphicsfairy); Giovanni Dall'Orto, "Il giardino 4" (2012, CC, Wikimedia); David Brewster, fig 33-36 "diagrams of the patterns of polycentral kaleidoscoped" (1819, Treatise on the Kaleidoscope); p.15: Carl Larsson, "Nu" (1914); Pearson Education—Scott Foresman, "Azalea" (CC, Wikimedia); photo of unknown man at beach; p.15 & 51: Pearson Education—Scott Foresman, "Seahorse" (CC, Wikimedia); p.16: Sophie H. Loury, "The Echo" (1895); p.18: John Singer Sargent, study for "The Archers" (ca.1910); pp.18-19: Mark Catesby, "Red Curlew (Eudocimus ruber.)" (c.1731-1743); p.19: ; p.22: Kristian Zahrtmann, "Adam i paradis" (1914); p.24: unknown artist, fig 19 "Skull and Lower Jaw of Dinictis" (1905, The American Museum Journal, v. V); p.26: Giovanni Boldini, "The Pianist Alexandre Rey Colaço at the Piano" (unknown date); Egon Schiele, "Raised Red Hand" (1910); p.26, 28, 84: 'Abd al-Hādī ibn Muhammad ibn Mahmūd ibn Ibrahīm al-Marāghī, "Swallows Flying" (13th century, Manāfi'-i hayavān); p.28: František Kupka, "The Yellow Scale (Self-portrait)" (1907); p.34: F. Edward Hulme, "Crocus" (1907, Familiar Garden Flowers by Shirley Hibberd); Arian Suresh, "Aloa lactinea (Red Costate Tiger Moth)" (2016, CC, Wikimedia); p.35: rabbit illustration (graphicsfairy); pp.36-37: Ohara Koson, "Myna on Magnolia" (unknown date); p.37: unknown artist, "Honeysuckle (Lonicera species)" (Wellcome Library no. 22254i); p.38: Vincent van Gogh, "Cypresses" (1889); pp.38-39: Anton Ažbe, "Study of a man" (1886); p.39: Carl Larsson, "Sunday Rest" (unknown date); Keramic Studio, honeysuckle illustration (1911); p.40: Plate LXXXI: "Head of Warrior, in British Museum" from Six Greek Sculptors by Ernest A. Gardner, M.A. (1910, Duckworth & Co.); p.42: Alireza Fazeli-Monfared, selfie (2020); p.43: unknown artist, "Magnolia conspicua" (1879, The American Cyclopædia, v. 11); p.44: Arkady Rylov, "Blue Explanse" (1918); p.48: Giovanni Dall'Orto, "L'indolente 3" (2010, CC, Wikimedia); William Sherwin, "Plate IV, features" (1685, Polygraphice); p.49: Pearson Education—Scott Foresman, "Tiger 2" (CC, Wikimedia); p.50: Pearson Education—Scott Foresman, "Conch" (CC, Wikimedia); pp.52-53: Dionisis Christofilogiannis, "Cyparissus with the deer" (2010, CC, Wikimedia); p.54: Thomas Eakins, "Thomas Eakins in Swim Suit" (1880s) Ulisse Aldrovandi, "Mostro alato con quattro braccia" (1642, Monstrorum historia); p.56: unknown artist, "Cicindela striolata (Tiger Beetles)" (1912, Coleoptera: General Introduction and Cicindelidaw and Paussidae by W.W. Fowler); František Kupka, "The Musician Follot" (1911); p.58: John Towner, "Storms at Sea" (2016, CC via Unsplash); Jacob Walti, photo of man underwater (CC via Unsplash); p.59: unknown artist, "Tiger lily (Lilium lancifolium)" (Wellcome Library no. 21902i); p.60: Thomas Eakins, "Talcott Williams, Thomas Anschutz, and J. Laurie Wallace" (detail of Talcott Williams only) (1883); p.62: Thomas Eakins, "J. Laurie Wallace and Talcott Williams" (detail of Talcott Williams only) (1883); p.66: unknown artist, "Gray Striped Tiger with Pine and Magpie" (unknown date); p.70: publicity photo of Robert Q. Lewis (1956); Bruno, "Magnolia grandiflora" (1892, Dictionnaire pratique d'horticulture et de jardinage by G. Nicholson); p.71: George S. Harris & Sons, "Dromedary" (1888, Wild Animals of the World series (N25) for Allen & Ginter Cigarettes); p.72: hummingbird illustration (graphicsfairy); unknown artist, "Flower of Honeysuckle" (1885, The Popular Science Monthly, v. XXVII); unknown artist, "Honeysuckles" (1889, The Canadian Horticulturist, v. XII n. 6); p.73: Wilhelm von Gloeden, n.0091 "Ritratto di giovane" (1890s); p.76: Albert Edelfelt, "Old Man Seated, Academic Study" (1874-1875); p.79: Louisa Anne Meredith after Henry Constantine Richter, "Thylacinus cynocephalus" (1881); J. Wolf, "Thylacinus cynocephalus, juv" (1848-1860, Proceedings of the Zoological Society of London Illustrations); Wyman & Sons Limited, "Thylacine" (1896, A Hand-book to the Marsupialia and Monotremata by Richard Lydekker); p.80: Sims, "Magnolia x thompsoniana" (1820, Curtis's Botanical Magazine 47); p.81: Kristian Zahrtmann, "Studiehovede en face af en mørkhaaret mandlig model—dagslys fra venstre side" (1867); p.84: John Singer Sargent, "Drawing" (1917-1920); p.88: Paul Signac, "Portrait de Félix Fénéon" (1890); p.90: Albert Hertel, "Männlicher Rückenakt" (1864); p.92: A.W. Mumford, no.1500 "Goldenrod" (1914, Nature Neighbors by Nathaniel Banta et. al); p.96: John Singer Sargent, "Study for 'Astronomy'" (c.1921); p.98: William Bruce Ellis Ranken, "portrait de jeune homme portant un panier de marguerites sur la tête" (1930); pp.98-99: tulip illustration from Karlsruher Tulpenbücher by Margrave Karl Wilhelm (ca.1730); p.100: Edwin George Lutz, "Buttercups and Daisies" (1921, Drawing Made Easy: A Helpful Book for Young Artists); Édouard Vuillard, "Self-portrait, Aged 21" (1889); photo of Kevin & Kerith Hawkins

159

(from personal collection of the author); p.101: Fritz Quant, "St. Matthias' Abbey, Trier" (1919); Robert Lewis Reid, "Tiger Lily" (date unknown); shell illustration (graphicsfairy); Robert Flogaus-Faust, "Glacier crowfoot" (2014, CC, Wikimedia); photo of Otis Bigelow (1940s, CC, Wikimedia); p.102: Richard Roland Holst, "Drie tijgerlelies" (1938); p.104: Tiziano Vecellio, called_Titian, "Nymph and Shepherd" (1570-1575); p.106: Franz Marc, "The Tiger" (1912); p.107: Wilhelm von Gloeden, n.2419 "Ritratto" (1895-1900); unknown artist, fig 79 "Autocrates œneus" (1912, *Coleoptera: General Introduction and Cicindelidae and Paussidae* by W.W. Fowler); unknown artist, "Jangsaeng hwarakdo" (Joseon Dynasty); unknown artist, "Magnolia grandiflora" (1879, The American Cyclopædia, v. 11); p.111: orange moth (graphicsfairy); John Gould, "Pyrocephalus parvirostris" (1841, *Zoology of the Voyage of H.M.S. Beagle Part 3* by Charles Darwin); Yinan Chen, "Quetzalcoatlus" (2014, CC, Wikimedia); p.112: unknown artist, "South African Crowned Crane" (Wellcome Library no. 43177i); Paul Kane, "A Winter Scene in the Rockies" (1846); p.114: G. Spratt, "Amygdalus Communis" (CC, graphicsfairy); p.116: Martin Kassem, "Heraldic Tiger" (2017, CC, Wikimedia); Frances Benjamin Johnston, "Portrait of a woman, partially draped, seated on a sofa" (1900); pp.116-117: Jairo Dealba, selfie (2020, used with permission); Ramon Casas, "Xavier Gosé" (date unknown); p.118: feather (graphicsfairy); p.120: Thomas Eakins, "Wallace Posing" (c.1883); p.121: photos of author's arms; p.122: Keramic Studio, tiger lily illustration (1911); unknown photographer, "Elsa von Freytag-Loringhoven" (before 1923); Richard South, plate 89 "Scarlet Tiger Moth & Jersey Tiger Moth" (1907, *The Moths of the British Isles*); Glyn Philpot, "Sleeping" (1931); p.126: Jacob Toorenvliet, "Kyparissos" (ca. 1701); p.128: Wilhelm von Gloeden, n.0263 "Caino" (ca. 1902); p.130: Gyula Benczúr, "Narcissus" (1881); p.131: Wilhelm von Plüschow, n.0978 "Sito Lempertz" (ca.1890-1907); pp.132-133: P. Miotte, "Astronomy: a chart of the phases of the moon" (Wellcome Library no. 46388i); W.W. Denslow, golbin illustrations (1899, *Father Goose: His Book* by L. Frank Baum); p.134: clover (graphicsfairy); Hans Hoffmann after Albrecht Dürer, "Hare" (1528); pp.136-137: Lawrence Alma-Tadema, "The Roses of Heliogabalus" (1888, details); p.137: John Singer Sargent, "Studies of a man's head" (c.1875); p.140: Walter Hood Fitch, "Mango Tree" from The Botanical Magazine (before 1870); p.142: photo of author (from personal collection); pp.142-143: Mario Andrea Valori, "Inner Pulp of the Kiwi" (2012, CC, Wikimedia); p.143: Jan Autengruber, painting (title unknown) (1914); p.144: photo of Stan Tucker (from the collection of the author); Sebastian Münster, "Labyrinth of the Minotaur" (1598); Pearson Education—Scott Foresman, "Hereford Bull" (CC, Wikimedia); p.145: Pancrace Bessa, plate 44 "Acer psudoplantanus & Acer platanoides" from The North American Sylva by François André Michaux; p.148: Ytha67, "Antonio Nazaré en el patio de cuadrillas de la plaza de toros de Béjar el 8 de septiembre de 2013" (2013, CC, Wikimedia); hills & ditch illustration (graphicsfairy); p.149: Maria Prymachenko, "Ukrainian Bull" (1977, CC, Wikimedia); p.150: Giovanni Dall'Orto, "Reflections 1" (2012, CC, Wikimedia); p.151: Pearson Education—Scott Foresman, "Tiger" (CC, Wikimedia); pp.152-153: Luis Ricardo Falero, "Playing with the Tiger" (1877); p.156: John Singer Sargent, "Study of a seated male nude" (1916-1921); Ulisse Aldrovandi, "[Calidris pugnax]" (1599-1603); Thomas Eakins, "Portrait of Douglass Morgan Hall" (c.1899); p.157, back cover: commissioned artwork by Mousetivity (2020, rights held by Brian Fuchs); p.160: Laurits Tuxen, "Academic male nude" (unknown date).

161

ENDNOTES

1 William Carlos Williams, "Choral: The Pink Church"
2 Lord Alfred Douglas, "Two Loves" (1895 poem)
3 Rainer Maria Rilke (translated by Annemarie S. Kidder), "I Am Much Too Alone in This World, Yet Not Alone"
4 Orville Peck (Daniel Pitout), "Big Sky"
5 Abū Nuwās, "Love in Bloom"
6 Rumi, "Dance, when you're broken open"
7 Faegheh Atashin (Googoosh), "Che Zibaa Bood"
8 E. E. Cummings, "that melancholy"
9 Jeff Martin, "Until I See Your Face (HoldUp)"
10 Emily Salt, "We Can Build You"
11 Rhiannon Marie, "The Monster"
12 Ron Padgett, "The Goldberg Variations"
13 Joe Brainard, "Out in the Hamptons"
14 J. Patrick Lewis, "Tom Tigercat"
15 Genara Necos, "Baile en Nueva York"
16 Sylvia Plath, "The Rival"
17 Jarrod Hol, line written for this poem
18 Maggie Culver Fry, "The Wheels Keep Turning"
19 AC Benus, "Poem No. 34"
20 Jessica Drake-Thomas, "A Kind of Dying"
21 Lawrence Ferlinghetti, "The Canticle of Jack Kerouac"
22 Carl Braun Sennhenn, "Ubi Sunt Puellae"
23 William Blake, "The Tyger"

24 Chris Cotter, *Oedipus Rex*
25 Robert A. Cozzi, "Jill and Toby"
26 Rhiannon Marie, "Four Angry Days in October 1998"
27 Janet McAdams, "Tiger on the Shoulder"
28 Kenward Elmslie, "Poem for Joe Brainard"
29 Chitra Banerjee Divakaruni, "Tiger Mask Ritual"
30 Justin Ward, "Catfight"
31 Michael Noonan, "Pipe Dream"
32 Yusef Komunyakaa, "Snow Tiger"
33 Diane Glancy, "Tiger Butter"
34 Sylvia Plath, "The Rival"
35 Adam Cornford, "Your Time and You"
36 Michael Walsh, "Lovers At Night with a Quilt"
37 Jairo Dealba, "Love Sonnet"
38 Belle Hunt Shortridge, "When Thou Art Gone"
39 Peter Orlovsky, "City Lights"
40 Jesse Cale, "Heart's Harbor"
41 Daniel Baylis, "Sail Boat"
42 Ted Berrigan, "Train Ride"
43 Allen Ginsberg, "Early Fifties, Early Sixties"
44 Shane Allison, "Kiss Me, John Before Your Wife Comes Home"
45 Kake Huck "In Memory of a Poet"
46 Jairo Dealba, line written for this poem

47 Ezra Pound, "Ortus"
48 John Muir, Edwin Way Teale, Henry Bugbee Kane (2001), "The Wilderness World of John Muir", p.312, Houghton Mifflin Harcourt
49 Caroline Churchill, The Queen Bee, 1892
50 Scott Hightower, "My Father"
51 Max Asbeek Brusse, "A Reunion of Old"
52 James W. Farris, "On Sweetwater Creek"
53 Evan Cromwell, "Tiny Human Hands"
54 B.C Hudalla, "If I Had Ever Been Enough"
55 Christine Perez, line written for this poem
56 Jeff Martin, "Tame the Wildflowers"
57 Jairo Dealba, "On cloud in heaven still"
58 Lawrence Ferlinghetti, "After the Cries of the Birds"
59 Ted Berrigan, "Three Little Words"
60 Donald (Grady) Davidson, "The Tiger-Woman"
61 Cheryl Couture, unpublished collaboration with Brian Fuchs
62 Michael Noonan, "a fool's song"
63 Jennie Harris Oliver, "Lake Okverholser"
64 Ellen Bass, "Relax"
65 Melissa Ginsburg "Tigers"
66 William Carlos Williams, "The Clouds"
67 Jairo Dealba, "Tigers"
68 Charles Wright, "(We can come to terms with the heavens)"
69 T. S. Eliot, "Rhapsody on a Windy Night"

www.ingramcontent.com/pod-product-compliance
Lightning Source LLC
Chambersburg PA
CBHW051424090426
42737CB00014B/2813